IX 11/00 √5/01

Wi

MW00471995

JAN 27 2000

WITHDRAWN

Photo by Scott Weldin

Sally Wingert, R. Hamilton Wright and David Pichette in the Arizona Theatre production of "Private Eyes." Set design by Scott Weldin.

JAN 27 1998

PRIVATE EYES

BY STEVEN DIETZ

★

★

DRAMATISTS
PLAY SERVICE
INC.

PRIVATE EYES
Copyright © 1998, Steven Dietz

All Rights Reserved

CAUTION: Professionals and amateurs are hereby warned that performance of PRIVATE EYES is subject to a royalty. It is fully protected under the copyright laws of the United States of America, and of all countries covered by the International Copyright Union (including the Dominion of Canada and the rest of the British Commonwealth), and of all countries covered by the Pan-American Copyright Convention, the Universal Copyright Convention, the Berne Convention, and of all countries with which the United States has reciprocal copyright relations. All rights, including professional/amateur stage rights, motion picture, recitation, lecturing, public reading, radio broadcasting, television, video or sound recording, all other forms of mechanical or electronic reproduction, such as CD-ROM, CD-I, DVD, information storage and retrieval systems and photocopying, and the rights of translation into foreign languages, are strictly reserved. Particular emphasis is placed upon the matter of readings, permission for which must be secured from the Author's agent in writing.

The stage performance rights in PRIVATE EYES (other than first class rights) are controlled exclusively by the DRAMATISTS PLAY SERVICE, INC., 440 Park Avenue South, New York, NY, 10016. No professional or non-professional performance of the Play (excluding first class professional performance) may be given without obtaining in advance the written permission of the DRAMATISTS PLAY SERVICE, INC., and paying the requisite fee.

Inquiries concerning all other rights should be addressed to International Creative Management, Inc., 40 West 57th Street, New York, NY, 10019. Attn: Sarah Jane Leigh.

SPECIAL NOTE

Anyone receiving permission to produce PRIVATE EYES is required (1) to give credit to the Author as sole and exclusive Author of the Play on the title page of all programs distributed in connection with performances of the Play and in all instances in which the title of the Play appears for purposes of advertising, publicizing or otherwise exploiting the Play and/or a production thereof. The name of the Author must appear on a separate line, in which no other name appears, immediately beneath the title and in size of type equal to 50% of the largest, most prominent letter used for the title of the Play. No person, firm or entity may receive credit larger or more prominent than that accorded the Author; and (2) to give the following acknowledgment on the title page of all programs distributed in connection with performances of the Play:

The World Premiere of PRIVATE EYES was produced by
Arizona Theatre Company, Tucson/Phoenix, Arizona
David Ira Goldstein, Artistic Director   Jessica L. Andrews, Managing Director

Produced in the 1997 Humana Festival of New American Plays at
ACTORS THEATRE OF LOUISVILLE.

SPECIAL NOTE ON POEM

Excerpt from "Loving the Killer" from LOVE POEMS.
Copyright © 1967, 1969 by Anne Sexton.
Reprinted by permission of Houghton Mifflin Co. All rights reserved.

SPECIAL NOTE ON SONGS AND RECORDINGS

For performance of the songs, arrangements and recordings mentioned in this Play that are protected by copyright, the permission of the copyright owners must be obtained; or other songs, arrangements and recordings in the public domain substituted.

For Allison

ACKNOWLEDGEMENTS

Seattle Playwrights Alliance
Mark Chamberlin
Susan Rome
Suzanne Bouchard
Empty Space Theatre
Eddie Levi Lee
Liz McCarthy
Christopher Evan Welch
Steven E. Alter
Joe Hanreddy
Jon Klein

PRIVATE EYES was produced at the 21st Humana Festival of New America Plays at Actors Theatre of Louisville (Jon Jory, Producing Director) in Louisville, Kentucky, as part of their 1997 Humana Festival of New American Plays, on March 4, 1997. It was directed by Steven Dietz; the set design was by Paul Owen; the costume design was by David Zinn; the lighting design was by Ed McCarthy; the dramaturg was Liz Engelman; and the stage manager was Juliet Horn. The cast was as follows:

MATTHEW ....Lee Sellars
LISA...Kate Goehring
ADRIAN ....V Craig Heidenreich
CORY...Twyla Hafermann
FRANK..Adale O'Brien

PRIVATE EYES received its world premiere at Arizona Theatre Company (David Ira Goldstein, Artistic Director; Jessica L. Andrews, Managing Director), in Tuscon, Arizona, on May 3, 1996. It was directed by David Ira Goldstein; the set design was by Scott Weldin; the costume design was by Rose Pederson; the lighting design was by Rick Paulsen; the sound design was by Steven M. Klein; the dramaturg was Rebecca Million; and the stage manager was Dawn Fenton. The cast was as follows:

MATTHEW ....R. Hamilton Wright
LISA...Sally Wingert
ADRIAN..David Pichette
CORY ....Katie Forgette
FRANK ....Jeff Steitzer

During the play's run in Phoenix, the role of CORY was played by Marianne Owen.

PRIVATE EYES (under the title, THE USUAL SUSPECTS) was initially developed, as part of Arizona Theatre Company's GENESIS New play Reading Series in March of 1993. It was directed by Matthew Wiener, the dramaturg was Jim Leonard, Jr., and the cast featured David Ellenstein, Brigitta Stenberg, Bob Sorenson, Collette Kilroy, and Michael Dixon.

CAST OF CHARACTERS

MATTHEW — a man in his thirties
LISA — a woman in her thirties
ADRIAN — a British man in his early thirties
CORY — a woman in her late twenties
FRANK — a man *or* woman, fifty

TIME and PLACE

The present.

Various rooms in an American city.

SETTING

A rehearsal studio that can be transformed, quickly and simply, into a variety of other locales. This is a play predicated on surprise and misdirection, therefore the scenic elements of any given scene should convince us that what we are seeing is real, is "the truth" — until the story of the play reveals it to be otherwise.

I will eat you slowly with kisses

even though the killer in you

has gotten out.

— Anne Sexton

PRIVATE EYES

ACT ONE

Suggested music: Joe Jackson's rendition of "Is You Is or Is You Ain't My Baby?" — introduction only.*

As the introduction to the song ends, lights reveal:

A Rehearsal Studio.

In the middle of the room, a small round table and two chairs. At one end of the room, a long table cluttered with resumés, scripts in red folders, pencils and coffee cups. A small trash can is next to the table.

Matthew sits behind the table.

MATTHEW.   Next. *(Lisa enters, carrying a shoulder bag.)* Hello.
LISA.   Hi.
MATTHEW.   *(Rifling through the resumés.)* You are —
LISA.   Lisa. *(Hands him her resumé.)* Lisa Foster.
MATTHEW.   Have I seen you before?
LISA.   I don't think so.
MATTHEW.   Your face is awful.
LISA.   Umm, well —
MATTHEW.   *(Looking at her photo.)* Get a photo that does you justice. *(She stares at him.)* Well. Let's get started. *(She moves to

---

* See Special Note on Songs and Recordings on copyright page.

the center of the room.) You're reading Carol, yes?

LISA. Yes.

MATTHEW. Did you have a chance to look at the scene?

LISA. Yes.

MATTHEW. Good.

LISA. From the entrance?

MATTHEW. Yes. *(Lisa moves to a corner of the room. Looks back to Matthew.)*

LISA. Is there something you're looking for?

MATTHEW. Yes. Whenever you're ready. *(Pause. Then, using her script as a tray, Lisa enters the scene. She speaks to the [unseen] customer in the chair.)*

LISA. Hi. What can I get you to drink? *(Pause.)* Can I start you off with something from the bar? *(Pause.)* Wine. *(Pause.)* Beer. *(Pause.)* HELLO. *(Silence.)* Look. Why don't I give you a little more time? I have other customers who actually take their sunglasses OFF to read the menu and actually acknowledge my questions when I ask them — *(Starts off, stops.)* Oh, god. You're Derek Savage — no, right, that's okay, you don't have to answer. I understand. They'd mob you in here. Oh, god, Mr. Savage. I've seen all your — oh, god, I'm saying it. I always thought that if I met you I'd have something more original to say than "I've seen all your films and I'm a big —" Wow. What? *(Looks at her script, nods "Yes.")* Uh-huh. *(Looks at her script, shakes her head "No.")* Huh-uh. *(She stares at him and then ... blushes ... looks away.)* Thank you. Really. Well ... why don't I give you a little more time with the menu and then I'll — *(Looks at her script, shakes her head "No.")* Huh-uh. *(Turning the page in her script, nods "Yes.")* Uh-huh. *(She stares at him and then ... slowly covers her mouth with her hand.)* My, uh, food is up. I need to go and do some, uh, *waitressing,* so — *(She starts to go, but — something he has said stops her. She stares at him. She looks over her shoulder, around the room. Then she sits in the chair at his table, across from him. She extends her hand, and "shakes" with the air in front of her.)* Carol. Carol Davis. *(A pause, then Lisa lowers her hand and looks up at Matthew, expectant. He stares at her.)*

MATTHEW. Okay. Good. Thank you, Lisa. *(He makes some notes on a pad in front of him. She waits, hopeful for him to say some-*

thing more — but he does not look up. She gathers up her things and starts off.) Are you in a hurry?

LISA.   I thought you were done with me.

MATTHEW.   I'm not done with you. Have you ever waited tables?

LISA.   *(Setting her bag down.)* Umm....

MATTHEW.   *Umm?* There's no umm here. This is a simple question. Have you waited tables or not?

LISA.   Well, I —

MATTHEW.   People think there are things I want to hear. I don't know where they get that notion. I ask direct questions and then watch glaciers form on the faces of people that would eat me alive anywhere else. If we were at a bar and I introduced myself and asked if you'd ever waited tables, you wouldn't hesitate. You wouldn't try to read me for the proper response. You would say yes or no, wouldn't you?

LISA.   Yes.

MATTHEW.   And why do we think that is?

LISA.   Here you have power. Anywhere else you'd have none. *(Silence.)*

MATTHEW.   Let me try this one more time. Have you ever —

LISA.   No.

MATTHEW.   Good. Thank you for your honesty.

LISA.   You're welcome.

MATTHEW.   Truth is air. And air is precious around here.

LISA.   Do you want me to do it again?

MATTHEW.   Oh, yes. And this time I'm looking for a little something *more.* A stronger relationship between you and Derek Savage. A bit more *impact.* Don't you think that is needed?

LISA.   Absolutely.

MATTHEW.   That's lacking, isn't it?

LISA.   Yes.

MATTHEW.   And why do we think that is?

LISA.   We think maybe because right now he's a chair. *(He stares at her.)*

MATTHEW.   People think I have no sense of humor, but I actually — are you married?

LISA.   Yes.

11

MATTHEW.   But I actually do have a sense of humor. I think humor is vital, life-giving. I think humor is air.

LISA.   I thought truth was air.

MATTHEW.   Let's begin.

LISA.   With the chair again?

MATTHEW.   Don't you believe you can play a love scene with a chair?

LISA.   *(Setting her script down.)* I should just go —

MATTHEW.   Don't you believe we *project* our loved ones? Don't you believe we form a picture in our head and then cast that picture like a shadow onto the person we're with? Don't you think the lover we *imagine* is actually more real than the one that stands before us?

LISA.   *(Turning to go.)* You're not going to want me in your play —

MATTHEW.   I want to know this. *(Pause.)* Really.

LISA.   I don't think you're describing love. You're describing vanity. If you'd like me to play the scene as though it were *about* myself and my image of another person's *love* for myself, I can do that. But I think that's cheap. And hollow. And utterly insignificant.

MATTHEW.   But, perhaps that is acting. *(She looks at him, hard. Then she walks up very close to him.)*

LISA.   Acting is the cold hard fact that someone is standing in front of you and you look into their eyes and they want something from you — and you from them — and through some combination of bloodshed and eloquence you find your place with each other. *That* is acting. What you're describing is one person's ability to manipulate events around them and keep their hands clean in the process.

MATTHEW.   Doesn't that happen? Haven't you seen that happen?

LISA.   Yes, I have.

MATTHEW.   And what would you call that?

LISA.   Directing. *(He stares at her.)*

MATTHEW.   I'll read with you. *(He grabs a script and sits in the chair. He takes sunglasses from his pocket and puts them on.)* Whenever you're ready.

LISA. *(Entering.)* Hi. What can I get you to drink? *(Pause.)* Can I start you off with something from the bar? *(Pause.)* Wine. *(Pause.)* Beer. *(Pause.)* HELLO. *(Beat.)* Look. Why don't I give you a little more time? I have other customers who actually take their sunglasses OFF to read the menu and actually acknowledge my questions when I ask them — *(She starts off as he removes his sunglasses, and looks up at her. She stops.)* Oh, god. You're Derek Savage — no, right, that's okay, you don't have to answer. I understand. They'd mob you in here. Oh, god, Mr. Savage. I've seen all your — oh, god, I'm saying it. I always thought that if I met you I'd have something more original to say than "I've seen all your films and I'm a big —" Wow.

MATTHEW. *(A British accent.)* Welsh.

LISA. What?

MATTHEW. Your family. Welsh, a little Scottish, a dash of Brit. Close?

LISA. *(Nodding "Yes.")* Uh-huh.

MATTHEW. And maybe, way back, some German.

LISA. *(Shaking her head "No.")* Huh-uh.

MATTHEW. Well, your ancestors did you proud. You are drop-dead gorgeous.

LISA. Thank you. Really. *(Pause.)* Well, why don't I give you a little time with the menu and then I'll —

MATTHEW. Are you married?

LISA. *(Shaking her head "No.")* Huh-uh.

MATTHEW. Boyfriend?

LISA. *(Nodding "Yes.")* Uh-huh.

MATTHEW. See that he worships you. Settle for nothing less. *(She stares at him, caught in his gaze.)*

LISA. My, uh, food is up. I need to go and do some, uh, *waitressing,* so —

MATTHEW. Why don't you join me? *(She stares at him, glances around the room.)* Let people talk. They can't touch us. *(He pulls back her chair from the table and she sits. He sits across from her. Extends his hand.)* Derek. Derek Savage. *(She shakes it, saying —.)*

LISA. Carol. Carol Davis. *(They hold hands for a moment, then Matthew pulls away.)*

MATTHEW. Now, I believe you.

LISA. What's that?

MATTHEW. Now I believe you've never waitressed. *(He quickly returns to his table, shuffles papers.)*

LISA. So, that wasn't what you were looking for?

MATTHEW. People don't know what they're looking for. They just know they're *looking.* Well, thanks for coming in — *(Reading the name off her resumé.)* Lisa. *(He tosses her resumé into the trash can. He speaks, brightly.)* We've done our work. It's lunchtime. *(Suggested music: "Is You Is or Is You Ain't My Baby?"** — *instrumental break. Lights shift to:*

A RESTAURANT.

A small table with two chairs. Matthew sits, alone. He lifts a menu from the table, looks at it, checks his wristwatch, waits. Lisa enters, now wearing a waitress apron. She stops for a moment when she sees him — then approaches the table. She stands near him, pen at the ready. Music fades out.)

LISA. Hi. What can I get you to drink? *(He looks up, sees her.)*

MATTHEW. Wait a minute. You said you —

LISA. I lied. Something from the bar?

MATTHEW. You work here?

LISA. Not according to my manager. Do you need a little more time?

MATTHEW. I — uh — no, I'm in a hurry.

LISA. Okay, shoot. *(He stares at her, disbelieving. Then he turns to his menu.)*

MATTHEW. How's the salmon?

LISA. Very good.

MATTHEW. And the linguine?

LISA. Very good.

MATTHEW. I see. What about the veal?

LISA. Very good.

MATTHEW. I suppose the entire menu is very good.

LISA. Yes. Very good.

MATTHEW. And would you tell me if something wasn't?

* See Special Note on Songs and Recordings on copyright page.

LISA. No, I would not.

MATTHEW. A good waitress would tell me.

LISA. Exactly. Now, what do you want?

MATTHEW. Why did you lie to me?

LISA. That bugs you.

MATTHEW. Of course it does.

LISA. Why should it matter if a stranger lies to you?

MATTHEW. You're not a stranger.

LISA. We've seen each other twice.

MATTHEW. In ten minutes.

LISA. Let's pick a china pattern. *(She leaves.)*

MATTHEW. Hey. I need to order — *(He looks around. Looks at his watch. Lisa arrives with a glass of red wine. Sets it in front of Matthew.)* What's this?

LISA. Our best Merlot.

MATTHEW. *(Lifting his menu.)* I'm ready to or—

LISA. *(Taking his menu from him.)* You're in a hurry. I ordered for you.

MATTHEW. You can't do that.

LISA. Sure I can.

MATTHEW. Why?

LISA. I have power here. Get used to it. *(She stares at him.)*

MATTHEW. I'm not in a hurry.

LISA. You lied.

MATTHEW. I changed my mind.

LISA. There's a difference?

MATTHEW. Yes.

LISA. Do tell.

MATTHEW. So, you're married?

LISA. Ten minutes ago I was.

MATTHEW. And are you still?

LISA. *More so.*

MATTHEW. Let me ask you something —

LISA. Your food is up. *(She leaves. Matthew sips his wine. Stares front. Looks around. Looks at his wine. Pause. He picks up the small box of matches that is on the table. He shakes it and hears nothing. Fearing it is empty, he opens it and happily discovers that there is one match left. He lights it and lets it burn, staring at it. Blows it out.*

15

Then, using his knife, he scrapes some of the charred black match into his wine. He quickly hides the burnt match and wipes his knife clean, as — Lisa arrives with a covered food plate. Before she can unveil it, Matthew lifts his wine glass.)

MATTHEW. I have a problem.

LISA. That's obvious.

MATTHEW. My wine. It has specks in it. Black specks. I'll need to send it back.

LISA. That's our best Merlot.

MATTHEW. Specks.

LISA. Interesting. Why do we think that is?

MATTHEW. I'm Matthew —

LISA. I know who you are.

MATTHEW. I just wanted to say hello, officially.

LISA. *Officially?*

MATTHEW. Out of the context of work.

LISA. Work?

MATTHEW. The audition.

LISA. You call that work? You sit there and get paid for having opinions and you call that *work?*

MATTHEW. It's what I do.

LISA. Believe me, I'd really love to sit here and get paid to tell people whether I *like the way they eat.* Don't have to make the food, don't have to serve it, and don't have to eat it — I just speak my mind and, miraculously, day after day, everyone mistakes my *criticism* for *accomplishment.*

MATTHEW. I think you've made your —

LISA. *(Sitting in the chair across from him.)* "Frankly, your eating just doesn't work for me. I'm looking for something *more.* A stronger relationship between you and your breaded chicken. A bit more *impact.* Don't you think that's lacking?"

MATTHEW. I'd like to be alone now.

LISA. Believe me, *you are. (Referring to the covered plate.)* Careful, that's hot. *(Lisa leaves, taking the wine with her. Matthew watches her go. He uncovers the plate in front of him. The only thing on the plate is a new box of matches. He smiles a bit. He lifts the box and shakes it. It is full. Pause. Then, he dumps the matches onto the plate. He takes a pen out of his pocket. He writes something inside the empty matchbox. He replaces the cover on the plate, and sets the match-box on the table in front of him. Lisa arrives, carrying a new glass of red wine. She sets the wine front of him.)* Here we are. Is everything all right? *(They stare at each other. No shift in tone.)* Say it.

MATTHEW.   No. *(They stare at each other.)*

LISA.   I'm still married.

MATTHEW.   I know that.

LISA.   Are *you? (Matthew slides the matchbox across the table, to-ward her. She looks at him, looks at the matchbox, then lifts it. She shakes the box and discovers it's empty. She opens the box. She reads the writing in the box. She stares at him. Then, she drops the match-box on the table, turns and leaves, quickly, as — music play. Suggested music: "I Want You"* by Tom Waits.)*

MATTHEW.   Lisa, wait — *(She is gone. Matthew stares front. Then he stands, throws a few bills on the table, and prepares to go, as — Lisa reappears. She is wearing her coat and carrying her bag. They stand, facing each other. Music continues under.)* Are we leaving? *(Lisa nods.)* Where are we going?

LISA.   It doesn't matter. We're strangers. Wherever we go, we'll be alone.

MATTHEW.   Lisa, I don't know what I'm looking for here —

LISA.   But you know you're looking. Aren't you? *(She walks up very close to him. Looks in his eyes.)* Do this.

MATTHEW.   What?

LISA.   Lie to everyone but me. *(They stare at each other. Then, they prepare to kiss. As their lips are about to come together — Adrian's voice is heard from the audience.)*

ADRIAN.   Okay, great, let's take five. *(Music snaps out, as lights expand immediately to reveal:*

THE REHEARSAL STUDIO.

Adrian walks to the stage.)

MATTHEW.   Can't we finish it?

ADRIAN.   What, the kiss?

---

* See Special Note on Songs and Recordings on copyright page.

MATTHEW. Well, yes, of course the kiss. But the rest of it. The rest of the scene.

ADRIAN. I thought we could use a break.

MATTHEW. But, Adrian, how was that? Was that more of what you were looking for?

ADRIAN. Well, as I've said, Matthew, I don't know exactly what I'm —

LISA. He just knows he's looking. *(Matthew stares at Adrian, exasperated.)*

MATTHEW. I need coffee. Lisa, you want anything? *(She shakes her head, saying nothing. Matthew goes. Adrian sits, working, at the rehearsal table. Lisa stands alone in the center of the room.)*

LISA. That was a little obvious, don't you think?

ADRIAN. What?

LISA. Before the kiss. Just before the kiss.

ADRIAN. There are some things I still have control over. *(A long silence.)*

LISA. There was a time we'd have prayed for this.

ADRIAN. For what?

LISA. A room of our own. Without hiding, without keeping up appearances. *(Pause.)* Five unexpected minutes. *(Pause.)* What would we have done?

ADRIAN. With these minutes?

LISA. Yes.

ADRIAN. Taken advantage, I suppose. Used them up.

LISA. How?

ADRIAN. Lisa —

LISA. I want to know this. What would we have done?

ADRIAN. *(Pause, simply.)* We would have devoured each other.

LISA. Yes. *(Pause.)* And what will we do now?

ADRIAN. This. *(Silence.)*

LISA. He's never asked, you know. It amazes me. He's never just come out and asked.

ADRIAN. It's a plan of his.

LISA. It's a what?

ADRIAN. It is a quiet torture. *(Pause.)* Sorry.

LISA. Perhaps you'd rather he asked.

ADRIAN. I said I'm sorry. Let it be.

LISA. Perhaps every time I came home late, or every time he walked in the room and we changed the subject, or every time he answered the phone and you quickly hung up — all those times, maybe he should have *asked*. "Are you seeing Adrian behind my back? Are you doing something as passé as having an affair with your director? Don't you have more *imagination* than that?"

ADRIAN. Lisa, I'm not saying —

LISA. No, this is good. This is very good. You're actually *disappointed* that he never found out. Why? Did it rob you of a good scene? An eloquent defense of your actions?

ADRIAN. And your actions.

LISA. That's understood.

ADRIAN. Meaning?

LISA. In this equation, when I say you I mean *us*. We are tethered to this mess.

ADRIAN. So, it's a mess now, is it?

LISA. Yes. *(Pause.)* I'm sorry, but ... yes. *(Matthew's voice is heard from off — or — he opens the rehearsal studio door briefly. Lisa and Adrian jump a bit.)*

MATTHEW'S VOICE. HOW 'BOUT JUICE? YOU WANT SOME JUICE?

LISA. NO, THANKS.

ADRIAN. I keep imagining him finding out *now*. Asking you about it *now*. It would just be too ironic to get away with it for the better part of six weeks — and then have him discover us now that we're over. *(Pause.)* To find what we've been hiding after there's nothing left to hide. *(She stares at him.)*

LISA. You don't think there's anything left to hide?

ADRIAN. No.

LISA. Really?

ADRIAN. Really.

LISA. You think we can be an open book now?

ADRIAN. Lisa —

LISA. You think we're a *clean slate?*

ADRIAN. I just think we're on the other side of it.

LISA. Well, of course you do. Because after you tell us where to stand and how loud to talk, you hop on a plane and plop into bed in another city.

ADRIAN. Lisa, let's not —

LISA. Let's not what? You're gone, I'm here. That's not fantasy. That's fact. I wake up next to my husband, who I love and who I've chosen to be with — but *we are still here*. You and I. We are everywhere I turn.

ADRIAN. What can I do about that?

LISA. I don't know. I don't. But there was a time when I thought you could affect everything. *(A quiet realization.)* God, I really did. I thought that through sheer force of will you could bring order to us. I want that back.

ADRIAN. It's over, Lisa. We decided it's over. *(Pause.)* Didn't we?

LISA. *(Soft.)* Yes. *(He moves in close to her.)*

ADRIAN. So, we must act on that. We must move on. *(Pause, a bit uncertain himself.)* Musn't we?

LISA. *(Soft.)* Yes. *(Pause.)* Let's move on. *(Pause, still soft.)* Do you really think we can we do that? *(Adrian holds her, speaks softly.)*

ADRIAN. Yes.

LISA. Okay. *(Pause.)* Let's tell him. *(Silence. He stares at her.)* Well?

ADRIAN. *("Leese.")* Lis —

LISA. Let's do it. As soon as he comes through that door. Let's tell him.

ADRIAN. *(Moving away.)* Lisa, you're not making any sense —

LISA. We have nothing to hide. You've taught me this. *(She puts two chairs side by side, facing the door/exit which Matthew will enter from.)* C'mon. Sit with me. We'll do this together.

ADRIAN. You'd better think about this, Lisa. You'd better think about the consequences of this —

LISA. No more thinking. Life is not what we think, it's what we *do* — and it's time we did *this*.

ADRIAN. But you don't just come out and tell someone the *truth*.

LISA. You don't?

ADRIAN. Not if you've *gotten away with something*, no. You don't then turn around and *confess*.

LISA. *(Challenging him.)* Why?

ADRIAN. Because —

LISA. Yes — ?

ADRIAN. Because it's *disruptive!* Imagine a world in which people *needlessly confessed* — it would be BARBARIC. Believe me, honesty should not be an *afterthought.*

LISA. What then?!

ADRIAN. It should be a *last resort. (Lisa stares at him, hard. Then, she starts for one of the chairs.)*

LISA. I'll do it myself.

ADRIAN. Lis — *(Lisa sits. Adrian stares at her. Then, he moves to the chair next to her, hesitates, and finally sits — then immediately jumps to his feet.)* Enough. All right? ENOUGH. I know you're trying to make a point of some kind, but —

LISA. A point?

ADRIAN. Yes.

LISA. A *point?*

ADRIAN. Forget it.

LISA. Adrian?

ADRIAN. What?

LISA. You're sweating.

ADRIAN. I'm — well, of course I am, I'm —

LISA. You know why, don't you?

ADRIAN. Lisa —

LISA. Because this is the *fever* we were always looking for. Stolen moments, secret phone calls — all of them gave us that *fever,* that heightened and frightened pitch that we were aching for. And Matthew was always nearby. *(Yells offstage — or — throws open the door, briefly.)* WEREN'T YOU, MATTHEW?

MATTHEW'S VOICE. JUST A MINUTE.

LISA. *(To Adrian.)* That was crucial to the equation. If he'd been in South America we might have bored each other to tears. But, he was always in the other room, or waiting in the car, or just out to get a paper — and the *finite time* we had made every moment *burn.* But it was never as good as *now.* This, Adrian, is the *thing itself. (Pause.)* So, *sit.* We signed on for this, let's end it in style. *(Adrian slowly sits in the chair, once again. Lisa sits again, also. They wait in silence.)*

ADRIAN. Lis?

LISA. What?

ADRIAN. I love you.

LISA. *(Tenderly.)* It was sweet, wasn't it? *(Matthew enters.)*

MATTHEW. Okay, so I've been in the dark. I've been in the dark about this entire thing. And you've let me. You've let me stumble through darkness like an oaf in a cave. And perhaps you've said this to yourselves over time: "It's for his *own good.* Nothing good would come of him knowing more at this time. Let's do this for *him.* Let's keep a little *darkness* around him." And I thank you for that. For thinking of me with such regard. Because, it seems you've needed to get together quite often — sometimes even outside rehearsal, sometimes till very late at night — to make sure you were doing the *right thing* when it came to me. I'm in your debt for that. I truly hope that some-how, someday I can repay the both of you. *(Adrian and Lisa look quickly to each other, then say —)*

ADRIAN. Matthew —

LISA. Why don't —

MATTHEW. Now, you are at a crossroads. You must take the next step. I'm aware of this and I don't envy your situation. At this moment, it must be said, that, for the first time in my life, I am completely thrilled to be *me.* Because my position is the simple one here. I lie in wait for you to enact your plan and then, holding cards you have no idea about, I play my hand. It's almost too easy. It's virtual baby candy. But, it's here and let's just accept it, shall we? Say: "Yes."

LISA and ADRIAN. Yes.

MATTHEW. Good. One thing I ask of you. There is this *myth.* I'd like us to talk about it. The myth of which I speak is that of Telling the Truth Slowly Over Time. Now, this myth does have its proponents. They believe that the cold hard truth can, if ra-tioned out slowly over time like, say, *cod liver oil,* be made more palatable. Perhaps even made attractive.

Therapists do this. They are reluctant to come right out and say to a couple: "Tom, Jeanine, thanks for coming by today and here's my assessment of your relationship: It's *fucked.* Let it go. Say good-bye, divide up your stuff, and run for your lives."

Why are they reluctant to do this? It would make them *obsolete*. Their jobs *depend* on giving out the truth at a *slower rate than it is actually needed*. They claim, of course (and are never challenged, since it is our fate to bow to anyone holding a weapon or a Ph.D.), that they are doing this for the couple's "own good" — that they are giving them the truth at a pace they can "*handle*." But, push has come to SHOUT and here we are: *(He moves closer to them.)*

I urge you to take whatever truth is at your disposal and *divest it.* Cut it loose. All of it. Tell it fast and tell it now. It is not more *palatable*, it is not a *gift* to tell someone you love the slow truth, unless you happen to know they have a fondness for slow disease like, say, *cancer.*

LISA. Matthew —

MATTHEW. Our collisions with others are not measured events. They are *radical.* Our love and lust and all our aching wonder is radical. Affairs don't accrue methodically, they spring up like lightning — like lost tourists with cash in hand. They are *feverish.* They are *fast.* And if we try to come clean by Telling the Truth about them Slowly Over Time, we give birth to a *mutant truth.* A truth that bears no relation to the fierce hearts that we possess. *The truth we tell, and the way we tell it, must be as radical as our actions. (Pause.)* And so ... Carol, Derek, what have you got to say for yourselves? *(Silence. Adrian and Lisa lean forward in their chairs.)*

ADRIAN. *Who?*

MATTHEW. *(A big smile.)* It's delicious, isn't it?

LISA. What is?

ADRIAN. Derek and Carol? *(Matthew happily pulls some folded script pages from his pocket.)*

MATTHEW. I'm sure I paraphrased it terribly. But you get the gist of it. It enables Michael to really nail Derek and Carol for the affair they're having behind his back.

ADRIAN. It's a *new page?*

MATTHEW. Yes, came in the mail today. Bonnie is copying them. *(Pause.)* What's wrong? What did I miss? *(Lisa and Adrian look at each other, then jump to their feet and congratulate Matthew.)*

LISA. Nothing!

23

ADRIAN.   Right! That's great. Wonderful. We'll work it in after lunch. In fact, let's take lunch *now*. I'm starved.

LISA.   I'll just grab my bag. *(Lisa bolts from the room. Matthew approaches Adrian.)*

MATTHEW.   Adrian?

ADRIAN.   Hmm?

MATTHEW.   Are you okay?

ADRIAN.   Sure fine great. Why?

MATTHEW.   You look pale. Peaked. *(Pause.)* Ashen, I guess it is.

ADRIAN.   You really did that from memory?

MATTHEW.   I took a stab at it. It's good, isn't it? It's what the play needs.

ADRIAN.   Yes, I think it will work nicely.

MATTHEW.   It will shut the two of them up. It will force them to just sit there and confront their lies.

ADRIAN.   Yes.

MATTHEW.   Their deceit.

ADRIAN.   Yes.

MATTHEW.   Their arrogant belief that things can actually be hidden.

ADRIAN.   Yes.

MATTHEW.   Because they can't, really. Do you know what I'm saying, Adrian?

ADRIAN.   I think I do.

MATTHEW.   And you agree with me?

ADRIAN.   I think I do.

MATTHEW.   I think you'd better. *(Silence.)*

ADRIAN.   Well, I should get a copy of the new pages from Bonnie. *(Matthew opens the folded script pages and holds them up — showing them to Adrian. They are completely blank.)*

MATTHEW.   Adrian.

ADRIAN.   Yes?

MATTHEW.   There are no new pages. You know that. *(He crumbles the pages and tosses them to Adrian, saying, brightly.)* Well. We've done our work. Let's eat. *(Suggested music: "Is You Is or Is You Ain't My Baby"* — final chorus to end. Lights shift to:*

* See Special Note on Songs and Recordings on copyright page.

A RESTAURANT.

The same table and chairs are used, with a few added elements to distinguish this from the Rehearsal Studio "Restaurant." Matthew sits between Lisa and Adrian. They sip their wine. They each are strangely aware of how they all seem to be bringing their glasses to their mouths at the same moment. They each work, subtly, to remedy this. Song ends.)

LISA. It's good. *(Silence.)*

ADRIAN. What's good?

LISA. The Merlot. It's quite good. *(Pause.)* It's a little ... smoky. Sort of. It has a kind of —

MATTHEW. Lisa.

LISA. Hmm?

MATTHEW. Don't explain the wine. *(Cory, their waitress, enters. She has long black hair.)*

CORY. How's the wine? *(Lisa stares at Matthew.)*

MATTHEW. It's *fine.*

CORY. Good. What are you eating?

LISA. Maybe we should get three different things and share. *(The men both lower their menus and look at Lisa.)*

CORY. I'll check back. *(She starts to go.)*

MATTHEW. No, I think we're ready. Go ahead, Adrian.

ADRIAN. I'll have the special.

LISA. Two.

MATTHEW. Three.

CORY. Well, that was easy. Salads with those?

LISA, MATTHEW and ADRIAN. Sure.

CORY. Great.

ADRIAN. Dressing on the side.

CORY. Got it. *(Cory goes. Silence.)*

ADRIAN. I think it's going very well.

MATTHEW. You do?

ADRIAN. Yes.

MATTHEW. Good.

ADRIAN. I really do.

LISA. What?

ADRIAN.   Hmm?

LISA.   What's going very well?

ADRIAN.   The play.

LISA.   Oh, yes, right.

ADRIAN.   Don't you?

LISA.   Absolutely.

ADRIAN.   Yes.

LISA.   Very well. Don't you, Matthew?

MATTHEW.   It's a *disaster*.

ADRIAN.   Well, Matthew, if you —

MATTHEW.   At the core of the play (I'm just realizing this now, as we're about to open) at the core of the play is her search for disaster. *(To Lisa.)* Right, Lis? *(Lisa stares at him, blankly.)* In actuality, her affair is a rather *pedestrian* event that will have *dire* repercussions. But, the folly (and I love this, I do), the folly of her life is that she believes just the *opposite*. She believes her affair is an extraordinary event which will offer *danger without consequence*. She is searching for *disaster with immunity*. *(Looks at the two of them.)* Wouldn't you agree? *(Adrian and Lisa stare at him, as Cory returns.)*

CORY.   Good news and bad news. Which would you like first?

| ADRIAN. | LISA. | MATTHEW. |
| The good. | Whatever. | The bad. |

CORY.   Well. The bad news is that we just ran out of the special. The good news is that the owner is buying your lunch.

MATTHEW.   Why?

CORY.   Apparently you're his one millionth table. *(Cory blows a plastic noisemaker. She walks around the table and places paper party hats on their heads during the following. She also sets three noisemakers in the center of the table. Matthew, Lisa and Adrian put their hats on and wear them until noted.)*

ADRIAN.   What do you know.

CORY.   So, eat and drink till you drop. There'll be a photo later.

LISA.   A *photo?*

CORY.   For some piece in the *Times*. Congratulations.

ADRIAN.   Thanks.

CORY.   Now, what are you eating?

LISA. I'll need to look at the menu again.

ADRIAN. As will I.

CORY. *(Nods.)* I'll start you with your salads. *(She goes. Silence. Then, Adrian blows his noisemaker.)*

ADRIAN. One in a million.

MATTHEW. *(Also blows his noisemaker, looking at Adrian.)* What do you know.

LISA. Matthew, I wonder if —

MATTHEW. I'm going to the restroom. Excuse me. *(Matthew goes. They watch him go, unable to turn and look at each other. Finally....)*

ADRIAN. He knows.

LISA. I know he knows.

ADRIAN. *How?* Were we careless?

LISA. Worse. We were smug. No one gets away with smug. *(Silence. At the same time, they both reach for their wine. They stop. They take each other's hands. Adrian moves to the chair closest to Lisa. They look into each other's eyes.)* What is it?

ADRIAN. *(Softly, urgently.)* Lisa. It needn't be over between us.

LISA. Adrian....

ADRIAN. There are things I haven't told you. Things that — if they come to pass — could change *everything.* Our lives could begin anew.

LISA. What are you saying?

ADRIAN. I can't tell you more, just now. I'm sorry. But, in time — *(Suddenly, the amplified sound of clicking cameras, as — several Photographers [played by the Crew] enter and circle Adrian and Lisa, snapping numerous photos. Adrian and Lisa stand and hold each other — trying to hide, to bury their faces, as they yell at the Photographers.)* No — get out of here — I said no — do you hear me — not now —

LISA. *(Overlapping.)* Could you please not — stop it — I don't want my — stop it — *(The Photographers are gone as quickly as they appeared. Lisa and Adrian, realizing they're holding each other in public, quickly let go of each other and step back, away. Then they remember the party hats on their heads — and quickly remove them. Lisa speaks simply, resigned.)* We have amnesia. We forget what we know. *(Adrian returns to the table and sits. Lisa stands, alone.)* This time, we think, unlike *all* the previous anguish and innuendo, *this time* the good-byes will have a grace to them. They don't. They never will. *(Lights shift to another area of the Restaurant:*

A WAIT STATION.

Cory is there, busily putting three salads and three sides of dressing on a tray. Matthew approaches her, still wearing his party hat.)

MATTHEW.   Hi.

CORY.   Hi.

MATTHEW.   You're a very good waitress.

CORY.   I can die happy.

MATTHEW.   Restrooms this way?

CORY.   Right through there.

MATTHEW.   Thanks. *(Matthew does not move. He watches Cory.)*

CORY.   You need something?

MATTHEW.   What? Oh, no. I'm just … waiting.

CORY.   Okay. *(Her tray is ready. She starts to go.)* See you.

MATTHEW.   Cory.

CORY.   *(Stops.)* How do you know my name?

MATTHEW.   I asked the owner. Cory, can I ask you something?

CORY.   Be quick. I'm busy.

MATTHEW.   Have you been following me?

CORY.   *What?*

MATTHEW.   *(Smiles.)* I know that sounds weird. But wherever I go lately, I keep seeing you. It's weird.

CORY.   Why haven't I seen you?

MATTHEW.   I don't know. I was there. *(Removes his party hat, extends his hand.)* Matthew.

CORY.   *(Shakes his hand, still holding her tray.)* Rest easy, Matthew. I'm not following you. *(Pause.)* I should go — or was there something else?

MATTHEW.   What do you mean?

CORY.   You didn't come back here to use the restroom.

MATTHEW.   I didn't?

CORY.   I see it a lot. This is a very good place to escape from one's tablemates. Are they married?

MATTHEW. No.

CORY. Oh. They look married.

MATTHEW. How do you mean?

CORY. They — you know — share a look. They match up.

MATTHEW. I hadn't noticed.

CORY. Well, it's hardest to see in our close friends.

MATTHEW. She's my wife. *(Silence. Cory smiles a bit.)* So, what do you do when you're not waitressing?

CORY. Don't be clumsy. Really.

MATTHEW. I'm not being —

CORY. Don't do this here. If this is a come-on, don't do it here. Really.

MATTHEW. It was an innocent question.

CORY. Wow. An innocent question. Wouldn't that be something?

MATTHEW. *(Simply.)* Set the tray down, Cory. *(They stare at each other. Standoff.)*

CORY. One condition. Don't be stupid about this. Not here. Not anywhere. Okay?

MATTHEW. Okay. *(Cory sets the tray down.)*

CORY. I'm not really a waitress. I'm a writer.

MATTHEW. What are you working on?

CORY. Actually, I'm working on a book about the depression.

MATTHEW. So, you have an interest in historical material?

CORY. *My* depression. I'm writing a book about *my* depression.

MATTHEW. I see.

CORY. It's an *epic*. *(She drinks from a glass of water on the Wait Station. Matthew smiles.)*

MATTHEW. So you don't like it here?

CORY. Put it this way: we have an owner who's "initiation ritual" for new waitresses involves the *walk-in freezer* and the *mint vinaigrette*. But, I dealt with it.

MATTHEW. *(Curious.)* What did you do?

CORY. *(Deliciously.)* What would anyone do? I became friends with his wife. I told her everything and she threw him out on his ass. If he fires me, I sue him. Game, set, match.

MATTHEW.   I believe in that sort of revenge. What's the dressing?

CORY.   Creamy garlic and dill. *(He dabs one of the sides of salad dressing with his finger. He tastes it.)*

MATTHEW.   Strong.

CORY.   We like it that way.

MATTHEW.   I like the adventure of revenge, don't you? The fever of it.

CORY.   Say more.

MATTHEW.   You are suddenly in power in a situation where you've previously been powerless. *(He reaches in his pocket and removes a small, glass vial which is filled with yellow powder.)* Do you have a fork? *(She stares at him. Then she hands him a fork.)* Thank you. *(As Matthew speaks, he does the following: He takes one of the sides of dressing off the tray. He sprinkles some of the yellow powder onto the dressing. He mixes the powder into the dressing with the fork. He repeats this with the second side of dressing, as well.)* This is what you must know about my wife:

My wife loves her wedding ring.

Sometimes I wake in the morning and catch her lying in bed next to me, holding her hand in the air, admiring her ring in the sunlight.

My wife never removes her wedding ring, with one exception: to wash the dishes. She places it carefully on a ledge above the sink. Then, when the dishes are done, she weds the ring to her finger once again.

I imagine she may also take it off to have her affair.

Therefore, this is my picture of her infidelity:

My wife is at the sink, holding a big yellow sponge.

She is doing the dishes.

There is a man *directly behind her.*

He is *not* doing the dishes.

Water gushes into the sink.

Steam glazes the windows.

My wife's hair has fallen across her face.

Her hands are red and wet.

Her fingers furrowed from this prolonged immersion.

With this man directly behind her, my wife washes every
... last ... dish ... in ... our ... home.

Later, when I walk through the door, she looks up from
her chair and smiles. "How was your day?" she asks, rubbing
the lotion into her hands. *(Silence. Cory stares at him. He places
the second side of dressing back in its place on the tray.)* Have you
nothing to say? *(Cory lifts the third side of dressing.)*
CORY.   And the third one?
MATTHEW.   That one's *mine*. Please, don't mix them up. *(She
stares at the dressing, at Matthew.)* I like you, Cory. I hope our
paths continue to cross. *(He puts the vial in his pocket. He puts his
party hat back on — and leaves. Cory watches him go, as lights shift
back to:*

THE RESTAURANT TABLE.

Matthew arrives and sits.)
MATTHEW.   No food, yet?
LISA.   ADRIAN.
She must be busy.   I'm starving.
(Silence.)
LISA.   Took you a while.
MATTHEW.   I stopped and used the phone. Checked our
machine.
LISA.   Any messages?
MATTHEW.   Just Adrian. Saying he'd see you at rehearsal.
(Looks at Adrian, smiles.) And he did. *(Adrian does his best to re-
turn the smile. Silence.)*
LISA.   Matthew, I — we — have something we'd like to talk to
you about.
MATTHEW.   Really?
LISA.   Yes.
MATTHEW.   About the play?
ADRIAN.   Not the play, per sé. Not the play *directly.*
MATTHEW.   I see.
LISA.   Something the play has *nurtured.* Something it has
birthed.

MATTHEW.   Something good or bad?

LISA.   Something —

ADRIAN.   Complicated. Something —

LISA.   Rash.

MATTHEW.   I see. *(Matthew removes his hat, leans in, concerned. Cory appears at some distance behind the table. During the following, she stands there, with the tray that holds the salads and dressings. The others do not see her.)* It sounds *serious*. Are the two of you in any danger?

LISA.   I don't think so.

ADRIAN.   I hope not.

MATTHEW.   Well, if there's anything I can do, I hope you'll let me know. But, please, if you don't mind, fill me in a little. Even if it's uncomfortable, please try. I feel at this point the three of us are close enough to deal with nearly anything. Don't you agree? *(Cory approaches the table.)*

CORY.   Here we are. Sorry about the wait. It's odd — but all the phones have gone out. It's total chaos back there. Reservations are all messed up. It's quite a scene. I hope no one needed to use the phone —

MATTHEW.   *(Smiles.)* Already did, thanks. *(Cory serves the salads. First to Lisa, then Matthew, then Adrian.)*

CORY.   Three salads. Three sides of dressing. It's our creamy garlic and dill. We get a lot of comments on it.

LISA.   Thank you.

ADRIAN.   Looks great. I am *starved*. *(Cory looks down at the three dressings. Stops. Uncertain. Then, she quickly — inexplicably — switches Matthew's dressing with Lisa's. Satisfied, she carries on, as Matthew looks up at her, concerned.)*

CORY.   *(Brightly, to Lisa.)* Fresh ground pepper?

LISA.   Please.

CORY.   Say when. *(Cory grinds pepper onto Lisa's salad.)*

LISA.   When. *(Cory stops, turns to Matthew.)*

CORY.   Fresh ground pepper?

MATTHEW.   *Please.*

CORY.   Say when. *(Cory grinds pepper onto his salad.)*

MATTHEW.   When. *(Cory stops. Before she can turn to Adrian, he says —)*

ADRIAN.   You bet. *(Adrian smiles, flirting with her.)* Shall I say *when?*

CORY.   Just tell me when you can't take it anymore. *(Adrian laughs. Cory grinds pepper onto his salad. At first, he smiles.)*

ADRIAN.   When when when when — *(She keeps grinding.)*

CORY.   You know what to say.

ADRIAN.   That's plenty, it's perfect, thank you — *(She keeps grinding. He's not smiling now.)*

CORY.   Can you not take *direction?*

ADRIAN.   That's enough —

CORY.   *Say it.*

ADRIAN.   I CAN'T TAKE IT ANYMORE. *(She stops and smiles, pleasantly.)*

CORY.   Can I bring you anything else?

MATTHEW.   I think this will do nicely. *(Cory goes. Adrian shakes the pepper off some of his salad.)*

LISA.   She looks familiar.

ADRIAN.   Our waitress?

LISA.   Yes.

MATTHEW.   I thought so, too. *(A frozen moment — the three of them looking off in the direction Cory left. Then, they each grab their sides of dressing and — using their forks — noisily cover their salads with dressing. Adrian stabs his fork into a huge piece of lettuce covered with dressing and is about to put it in his mouth.)*

LISA.   Adrian?

ADRIAN.   What?

LISA.   Wait. We're in the midst of something. Let's finish it.

ADRIAN.   Lisa —

LISA.   Let's get it said. *(He looks at her, then lowers his fork.)* Matthew?

MATTHEW.   Yes?

LISA.   *Something happened.* Something between Adrian and me.

MATTHEW.   Yes, so I gather. *What was it?* I'm dying to know.

LISA.   Well, it's —

ADRIAN.   Enough. I'll do this. *(He sits up straight, looks Matthew in the eye.)* Matthew, your wife and I —

MATTHEW.   Adrian.

ADRIAN.   Yes.

33

MATTHEW. Before you go on, I must tell you one thing.

ADRIAN. *(After a glance at Lisa.)* All right.

MATTHEW. You look *famished*. We can't afford you to get sick. Not this far into rehearsal. Let's, please, eat while we talk. Let's, please, chat and chew. *(Adrian and Lisa look at each other. Matthew takes a huge bite of his salad. Adrian and Lisa then take huge bites of their salads. Cory is seen once again, watching from a distance.)* Mm-mmm. There. I feel better already. Now, Adrian, what were you saying?

ADRIAN. Well, Matthew, in plain terms, your wife and I — *(He stops, choking a bit. Distant, eerie music is heard, under.)* Your wife and — *(He chokes more.)* I can't seem to — *(More choking, coughing.)* OH GOD — *(Choking violently.)* OH GOD, HELP ME — *(Lisa stands and steps toward Adrian, trying to help.)*

LISA. Adrian, what is it? Adrian! Here, drink something — *(Now, Lisa, too, coughs. She quickly grabs her own throat, choking to death.)* Oh … my … god —

ADRIAN. *(Desperately, to Cory.)* CALL FOR HELP — CALL 911 —

CORY. *(Smiling, holding the severed end of a pay phone.)* Phone's are dead! Sorry!

LISA. MATTHEW —

MATTHEW. *(Happily.)* Your face is blue, honey. And you know what? It's a *very good* color on you!

LISA. MATTHEW, *DO SOMETHING* —

MATTHEW. Okay! *(Matthew stands atop the table and snaps his fingers, as — loud music suddenly plays. Suggested music: "Tell the Truth"* by Ray Charles, and — The stage is suddenly flooded with pulsating green and red light. A mirror ball [perhaps] spins, above. Spotlights [perhaps] hit Matthew atop the table and Cory, standing now atop the Wait Station counter — Matthew and Cory watch and laugh and dance to the music, as — Adrian and Lisa scream in pain, cough, choke and throw themselves around the room. Lisa reaches up, desperately, for Matthew — just as he jumps down from the table. She pulls the tablecloth from the table and salad flies everywhere. Total chaos — the Photographers — now wearing party hats — rush on and*

---

* See Special Note on Songs and Recordings on copyright page.

quickly take photos of Adrian and Lisa clinging to each other's necks as they choke and die — the amplified sound of manic laughter joins the music — Matthew climbs atop The Wait Station, as Cory puts a long red rose between her teeth. Matthew dips her dramatically, and — as she takes the rose from her teeth — he kisses her, passionately, as — the Photographers capture the kiss on film, then rush off, as — Lisa and Adrian finally die, hideously, as — Matthew stands over them, laughing wildly, and — Cory blows kisses and waves good-bye to them — Then, suddenly — abrupt light shift. Music out. All action freezes. A person stands at the edge of the stage in a shaft of light, holding a clipboard with paper, looking at Matthew. This is Frank. A similar shaft of light isolates Matthew.)

FRANK. *(Dryly.)* Matthew?

MATTHEW. Yes?

FRANK. Did that really happen? Is that really what you did? *(Silence.)*

MATTHEW. It's what I *wanted* to do.

FRANK. There's a *difference*, Matthew. We've been over this.

MATTHEW. *(Pause.)* I'm sorry, Frank.

FRANK. You owe me no apologies, Matthew. You only owe me the *truth*. That's the only way I can help you. *(Frank makes a note on the clipboard.)* I think we should add a *second session* each week. And I think we need to go *back*, Matthew. Back to the very beginning. Is that clear?

MATTHEW. *(Soft.)* Yes, Frank.

FRANK. Good. *(Brightly.)* Well, we've done our work. It's lunchtime. *(Fast blackout. Suggested music: Something like "Can I Steal a Little Love?"* sung by Frank Sinatra.)*

END OF ACT ONE

* See Special Note on Songs and Recordings on copyright page.

ACT TWO

Suggested music: "Fever"* — sung by Peggy Lee. Music snaps out as lights bump up on Matthew and Frank in positions identical to the end of Act One. The rest of the stage remains in darkness.

FRANK.   And I think we need to go back, Matthew. Back to the very beginning. Is that clear?

MATTHEW.   *(Soft.)* Yes, Frank.

FRANK: But first, Matthew, let's remind ourselves of our first meeting. Can we do that? *(Matthew nods. Lights expand to reveal:*

FRANK'S OFFICE.

Two comfortable chairs. Framed degrees and plaques on the wall. Matthew and Frank move to the Office and sit.)

FRANK.   Splendid. Now. When we first met, what did you say?

MATTHEW.   I said: "Hello."

FRANK.   Good. And what did I say?

MATTHEW.   You said: "I'm Frank. I hope *you'll* be."

FRANK.   Well, Matthew, that's my question: *have you been?* Or have I been the only one in the room being Frank? *(Matthew stands.)*

MATTHEW.   Watch. I'll show you how it started. *(The Rehearsal Studio. Two scripts in red folders neatly stacked on the table. [Note: These are identical to the scripts used throughout Act One.] Freshly sharpened pencils. A coffee mug. Adrian enters, briskly, carrying his script. Frank watches from the office, taking occasional notes.)*

ADRIAN.   You're early.

MATTHEW.   Yes, we had a —

ADRIAN.   *(Shaking his hand.)* Welcome aboard, Matthew! I'm greatly looking forward to the next six weeks. I think we're in for a splendid adventure. The company I run in London has

---

* See Special Note on Songs and Recordings on copyright page.

often tackled projects of this magnitude and I quite fancy the chance to bring my aesthetic to America — to the *provinces*, if you will. As soon as Lisa gets here, we'll make a start.

MATTHEW. She's here.

ADRIAN. Really?

MATTHEW. She came with me.

ADRIAN. Really?

MATTHEW. She's my wife. *(Adrian smiles.)* Really.

ADRIAN. I must say I didn't know that. *(Pause.)* Well, congratulations. *(Before Matthew can respond.)* Don't say it. Don't say "thank you." I withdraw my comment of congratulations. Please forgive me, would you? I entreat you —

MATTHEW. Forgive you?

ADRIAN. That's trophyism, don't you think? "Congratulations on your wife" — that's trophyism, it's caveman talk. It shouldn't be thought of as an *accomplishment* that someone landed a strikingly beautiful woman as his wife.

MATTHEW. What should it be thought of as?

ADRIAN. What it more accurately *is*.

MATTHEW. And that is?

ADRIAN. Envy. *(Pause, brightly.)* Well, I've broken a few Commandments and I haven't even had my tea. Excuse me. *(Adrian goes, taking his coffee mug with him.)*

FRANK. *Matthew?*

MATTHEW. It *happened*, Frank. I swear it. You said you wanted to go back to the beginning. Well, here we are.

FRANK. Very well. Keep going. *(Lisa enters, then stops — staring back at the door/entrance she came from. Frank continues to watch.)*

MATTHEW. Lis.

LISA. Hmm?

MATTHEW. Are you okay? *(Lisa turns to Matthew. She goes to him and puts her arms around him, tightly.)*

LISA. He just said the strangest thing to me.

MATTHEW. Who?

LISA. Adrian. Just now, we passed in the hallway, and he said hello, and then he said the strangest thing.

MATTHEW. What was it?

LISA. *(Pause.)* I can't tell you.

MATTHEW. Sure you can.

LISA. No.

MATTHEW. *(With a laugh.)* Lisa, I'm your husband, I'm your friend, you can tell —

LISA. No. He told me not to. He told me not to tell you. *(Adrian enters, carrying his still-empty mug.)*

ADRIAN. Let's jump!

MATTHEW. What?

ADRIAN. Let's jump to the end.

MATTHEW. To the —

ADRIAN. As a way of starting, I'd like to jump to the end.

FRANK. *(Making a note.)* Interesting.

ADRIAN. It's something I do with my company in London (where, of course, one can get a CUP OF TEA before rehearsal begins — but no such luck HERE, is there?) In any case, let's give the play's final scene a "once-over" and see where this thing *ends.* Are you game? *(Matthew and Lisa stare at him, then say ...)*

MATTHEW and LISA. Sure. *(Adrian sets a wooden chair in the center of the room. After placing it, he looks at it ... then changes the angle of the chair ever-so-slightly. Then he steps away from it and looks to Matthew and Lisa, expectant.)*

ADRIAN. Would you like to use the chair?

LISA. Do you want us to use the chair?

ADRIAN. That's not my question. My question is —

MATTHEW. *(Setting the chair aside.)* No. I don't want to use the chair. *(Adrian nods for a really long time, then says ...)*

ADRIAN. *Interesting.*

LISA. What is?

ADRIAN. That you don't feel a need to use the chair. That's *very telling.*

LISA. I doesn't really matter to me whether we — *(Matthew grabs the chair and sets it in the center of the room once again. Smiles.)*

MATTHEW. We're using it, all right? We're using the fucking chair.

ADRIAN.   Your choice. *(Adrian again adjusts the chair ever-so-slightly. Then he lifts the scripts from the rehearsal table and hands them to Matthew and Lisa.)* And one thing more: Please use your *real names.*

LISA.   When?

ADRIAN.   In the scene.

MATTHEW.   Not the character's names? Not the names in the *script?*

ADRIAN.   No. Your own.

MATTHEW.   But —

ADRIAN.   Matthew. This is how I work. *(Matthew stares at him, then nods, sits. Adrian gestures for Lisa to start on the opposite side of the stage.)* The final scene. At your leisure.

MATTHEW.   Are you going to tell us anything? Is there something you're looking for?

ADRIAN.   Of course there is. Now: the final scene. *(Prompted by a gesture from Adrian, Lisa walks slowly past Matthew who sits, reading. Lisa stops ... turns ... looks back at him ... their eyes meet. The scene is quiet ... lovely ... simple.)*

LISA.   Oh, my god.

MATTHEW.   Lisa. *(Stands.)* It's been —

LISA.   Years.

MATTHEW.   Yes. *(Pause.)* Four years. And you're still —

LISA.   Finishing your sentences. *(Matthew smiles a bit. Silence.)*

MATTHEW.   So, it worked out. Your marriage?

LISA.   *(Pause, gently.)* Yes.

MATTHEW.   I'm glad for you. *(Pause, quietly.)* Really.

LISA.   And you?

MATTHEW.   Nothing to report.

LISA.   *(Tenderly.)* Four years? *(Matthew nods.)* And there's been no —

MATTHEW.   Only you.

LISA.   Matthew —

MATTHEW.   This is what happens, Lis. Someone always wakes up first. *(They look into each others eyes — then, simultaneously, turn the pages of their scripts.)*

LISA.   I should go. My husband is picking me up.

MATTHEW.   Just like old times. *(She nods.)* Something I've wondered.

LISA. What?

MATTHEW. Did he ever — did you ever —

LISA. No. Never. *(Pause.)* It's still our secret. *(Pause.)* Good-bye, Matthew. *(Lisa goes, exiting to the side of the stage. Then, Lisa and Matthew turn and look at Adrian. Adrian is staring intently at the chair, nodding his head, slowly and repeatedly, for a really long time. Finally, Lisa says ...)* Well? *(He looks up at her. Speaks, softly.)*

ADRIAN. That *is* what happens, isn't it? I've never known that as fully as I do now. Someone *must*, of course, wake up first. And the shock is that we mistakenly believe we will recognize the END as *mutually* as we recognized the BEGINNING. But we are offered no such elegance. *(From his heart.)* Because ... when, in a marriage ... when, in a life.... *(Stops.)* No. No more. *(Adrian has settled into the chair, his head in his hands. Lisa and Matthew look at each other. Then, Matthew tentatively approaches Adrian.)*

MATTHEW. So ... what we did was *okay?*

ADRIAN. *(Standing with a flourish.)* It was a *revelation.* It gave me a clarity of purpose about my own life — well, need I say more, you're married, you know what a circus of neurosis it can be, of course you do — but let's dispense with confession and attend to business at hand.

MATTHEW. But, just so I'm clear: That's what you want — you want us to do the scene that way?

ADRIAN. Matthew, it's not the scene that matters — it's the *art.* And, in the end, what is art, what is LIFE, but this?: A bit of love ... a few laughs ... and then ... *death. (Pause. Then, brightly.)* Take ten, please. *(Matthew goes directly to Frank, as lights expand to include:*

FRANK'S OFFICE.

During the following, Adrian goes through his script, making nota-tions. Lisa sits, across the room from Adrian. She removes a thermos from her bag. Pours herself some tea.)

MATTHEW. *That*, Frank, is how it began.

FRANK. May I see your script, Matthew?

MATTHEW. My — ?

FRANK. It may provide a clue to our work. *(Hand extended.)* May I? *(Matthew hands Frank his script. Frank pages through it during the following.)* Now, what happened next?

MATTHEW. I went outside to smoke.

FRANK. You don't smoke, Matthew.

MATTHEW. So, I came right back in. And that's when I heard her say:

LISA. Adrian? *(Adrian looks up at Lisa.)* Would you like some tea? Everyone around here is a coffee drinker, but not me. *(She lifts the thermos, offers it.)* English breakfast. Will you have a cup? *(Adrian nods. She walks to him and pours him some tea. Frank puts the script aside.)*

FRANK. And then?

MATTHEW. And then it began.

FRANK. What did?

MATTHEW. *Them.* The two of them.

FRANK. But how do you know? Did you *observe something?*

MATTHEW. Not right then — no — we were on a break, so I turned and left —

FRANK. She did nothing but offer him a cup of tea. That's all you know for sure, Matthew, and I don't think —

MATTHEW. You know, I thought I was paying you to *believe what I say.* Do you now want *proof?* Do you now want hair fibers? Surveillance photos? An affidavit from a private detective?

FRANK. Do you have one?

MATTHEW. Forget it — I'm going for a smoke.

FRANK. But, Matthew, you don't —

MATTHEW. It's a FIGURE OF SPEECH, Frank. I'll see you Friday. *(Matthew leaves. Frank watches him go, then turns back to:*

THE REHEARSAL STUDIO.

Lisa and Adrian are sitting across the room from each other. They sip their tea. Lisa reads a newspaper. Adrian makes the occasional note in his script.)

FRANK. Odd. How brutal things begin so sweetly.

How our greatest regrets take root, at first, as hope. *(Frank turns and addresses the audience.)*

Pardon me for addressing you directly, but it seems I'm the only one who can be trusted with this story.

It's possible, of course, that what Matthew said is true. That it began between them on that day, at that moment.

But, *why?* I am asked that often. And, frankly, I've come to believe that each reason is as plausible as the next. One client assured me her affair was caused by the curvature of the earth. What could I say? Did I know otherwise?

So, tonight, I ask it of you. *Why?*

You've all seen that person who caught you off-guard. Who stopped your breath, if only for a moment. That person you walked a little faster just to get a glimpse of. Or slowed your car ever so slightly to observe. And why? Just to *see.* Just to *take it in.*

Perhaps this was years ago when you were young and hopeful and reckless. Perhaps this was at intermission.

But, however brief, that glance *registered.*

And you put it somewhere in your mind.

And that ... may have been that.

LISA.   There's a hurricane coming.

ADRIAN.   *(Looking up from his work.)* What's that?

LISA.   Oh, I'm sorry. It's a terrible habit. I do it at home all the time and it drives Matthew crazy. I'm a blurter. Sorry.

ADRIAN.   You're the person who ruins the newspaper for everyone in the room.

LISA.   That's me. Sorry. *(The tea.)* Is your — ?

ADRIAN.   *(Lifting his cup.)* It's lovely. *(Lisa goes back to her paper. Adrian keeps looking at her.)* What are they calling it? *(She looks up at him.)* The hurricane.

LISA.   Cory.

ADRIAN.   *(With a laugh.)* Say again?

LISA.   Hurricane Cory. Is that a man or a woman, do you suppose?

ADRIAN.   Woman. Definitely a woman.

LISA.   How can you be sure? *(Adrian just smiles and goes back to his script. Silence, as Lisa stares at him.)* Thank you for casting me in this.

ADRIAN. *(Head in script.)* My pleasure. You were my first choice.

LISA. Really?

ADRIAN. *(Not looking up.)* Mm hmm. *(Silence. Lisa watches Adrian as he makes some marks in his script.)*

LISA. *(Simply.)* You're sort of a prick, you know. *(He looks up at her.)* Have people told you that? It's not that you're British — its not that at all, in fact, that's a large part of your charm — no, it's — I think its just your — well, just your style. Your manner. You come off as, well — as a sort of —

ADRIAN. Prick.

LISA. Okay, that may have been too harsh. I didn't —

ADRIAN. No, you said "Prick" and in my experience "Prick" is not a word that people just pick out of the air *casually*. It's a word that one *reserves;* an arrow kept in one's quiver till the proper target is found.

LISA. Adrian —

ADRIAN. No. Don't you dare. Don't you dare back down from this.

LISA. I'm not planning on backing down from it, I just —

ADRIAN. *(Approaching her.)* What then? What are you planning?

LISA. Look. This didn't go well, why don't we —

ADRIAN. What makes you think it didn't go well? We've done something *amazing* here, can't you see that?

LISA. What are you —

ADRIAN. We've jumped. It's delicious, isn't it? To not wade in. To not build a rapport slowly and predictably — brick by brick, anecdote and response — but, instead, to leap past the introductions, leap past the formalities and into — *(He stops.)*

LISA. What? Into what?

ADRIAN. We've only six weeks together. We must move with dispatch.

LISA. Translate:

ADRIAN. Quickly. *(He stares at her.)*

LISA. Adrian —

ADRIAN. When you auditioned for me, I didn't hear a word you said. Forgive me, but I was looking at your neck, your body — and my mind took off to a time and place I'd long forgotten.

LISA. *(Looking in the direction Matthew exited.)* He's just outside, you know. He'll be back in a —

ADRIAN. It's a chance I'll take.

I was fifteen years old. In the summers, I worked at a market — cleaning and gutting fish all day, packing them in ice. The stink of fish on my hands, in my hair, all summer. The stray cats everywhere.

At lunch, I'd sit outside and look across the street. And there, nearly every day, was a young woman hanging clothes on a line to dry. A light summer dress. Short, red hair. And each day, I'd watch her. Her body. Her neck — the way it held up her head like an offering. The breeze rippling her dress. I'd sit and watch the way she moved (like God's own dream), the cats licking at my fingers. *(Silence. Lisa stares at him.)*

LISA. You're not a prick, Adrian. If you were, you wouldn't be dangerous.

ADRIAN. You think I'm dangerous?

LISA. Oh, yeah.

ADRIAN. To whom?

LISA. To no one but me. And that's the point, really, isn't it? *(She stands and approaches him.)* So, no, I won't back down. Even though I should. Even if you ask me to. *(Pause, close to him.)* What's your middle name? We're strangers till I know that.

ADRIAN. *(Quietly.)* Ross.

LISA. *(Quietly.)* Thank you. *(Matthew enters, holding his script.)*

MATTHEW. Well, what now?

LISA. *(Moving away.)* "Adrian Ross." I like that.

MATTHEW. Which scene are we working next?

ADRIAN. *(Paying no attention to Matthew.)* When do they expect her?

MATTHEW. Who?

ADRIAN. The hurricane.

LISA. Oh, not for a while. She's still at sea.

MATTHEW. Are we going back, or what?

ADRIAN. Actually, Matthew, I'd like to work on Lisa's monologues now —

MATTHEW. Fine.

ADRIAN. — So, why don't you go ahead and take lunch.

44

MATTHEW. I'll wait.

ADRIAN. You needn't.

MATTHEW. I'll wait for Lisa.

ADRIAN. That's not necessary.

MATTHEW. It's no problem. We'd rather have our lunch together, right Lis?

ADRIAN. *(Before Lisa can respond.)* It's a private moment, Matthew. I must insist that you leave us alone. Nothing personal, but ... this is how I work. *(Matthew looks at Lisa, then back to Adrian.)*

MATTHEW. Yes. I'm beginning to see that. *(Pause.)* Lis?

LISA. I'll meet you at the restaurant when I'm done. *(Matthew looks at her. Nods. Then, leaves. Frank enters the Rehearsal Room, speaking to the audience, as before.)*

FRANK. Most affairs, you see, are over within minutes. A daring glance, a brazen word — and it's done. We come to count on that.

ADRIAN. You'll need your script. *(Lisa picks up her script. She stands, waiting. Adrian remains distant, across the room.)*

FRANK. A delicious part of living in the world is the number of lives we *brush past* but never *enter*. The bonds we've created, the institutions we've built — not to mention the rigorous logistics of even the most banal infidelity — all these things serve to keep us on the straight and narrow.

ADRIAN. Do you know which scene we're doing?

LISA. Yes.

FRANK. *(Standing close to Lisa, looking at her.)* Every now and again, though, we let ourselves think ... *"What if?"* But, thankfully, the question itself can be counted on to stop us in our tracks.

ADRIAN. Do you know what I'm looking for?

LISA. Yes.

FRANK. Unless, of course, that question leads to another question ... *"How?"* And if we make it to "How?", well, we're only a stone's throw from *"When?"* *(During the following, lights isolate down to a pool of light on Lisa and a shaft of light on Frank. Adrian circles Lisa, slowly, then approaches her from behind. He stands directly behind her, very close. He does not touch her. She con-*

tinues to stare front, taking a deep breath ... with Adrian's face very near the back of her neck.) And at that moment, as we stand at the precipice of deceit ... we are grateful for the privacy of our fantasies. We revel in our ability to carry out sin *within the confines of our own mind* — leaving our life protected and our spouse unaware.

And having stood at that precipice ... our common sense returns. And we put aside our foolish notions. And that is that.

ADRIAN. Any questions before we begin?

LISA. *(Soft, still staring front.)* No.

FRANK. *Usually. (Lisa slowly closes her script ... turns ... and kisses Adrian on the mouth. Suggested music: "Don't Explain"* by Dexter Gordon.)* Unless the earth curves. *(Music continues, as lights shift to:*

THE RESTAURANT.

Matthew enters and stands near the table. He looks around for someone to seat him or wait on him — but, there's no one in sight. Cory enters, following Matthew at a distance. She now has short, red hair. She is wearing a black leather jacket, and dark sunglasses. She appears to be a different woman than we saw in Act One. Matthew decides to leave. As he turns, Cory coolly ducks out of sight. Matthew stops, changes his mind, and returns to the table. Sits. Cory approaches him.)

CORY. Excuse me — is anyone working here today?

MATTHEW. Not that I can tell.

CORY. None of the tables are bussed, and there's not a waitress in sight.

MATTHEW. I grabbed the only clean table I could find.

CORY. I see that. *(Music fades out.)*

MATTHEW. This place is usually packed. I've been coming here for two weeks.

CORY. You work nearby?

MATTHEW. I'm an actor. I'm in rehearsal down the street.

CORY. With Adrian Poynter?

---

* See Special Note on Songs and Recordings on copyright page.

MATTHEW.   Yes. You know him?

CORY.   I've followed his career.

MATTHEW.   Really? I didn't know he was well-known.

CORY.   It's relative, I suppose.

MATTHEW.   I suppose. *(Pause, stands, looks around.)* Well, this is ridiculous. I think I'll see if there's another —

CORY.   Would you like some wine?

MATTHEW.   You have wine?

CORY.   I was on a plane this morning. They left the cart near my row. *(From her jacket, she brings out two small airplane-size bottles of red wine.)* Join me? *(Matthew stares at her, then nods.)*

MATTHEW.   Sure. *(Cory sits at the table, across from him. She lifts her bottle, toasting.)*

CORY.   Here's to it.

MATTHEW.   To what?

CORY.   *(Removing her sunglasses.)* To truth at all cost. *(They clink bottles and drink. They sit in silence for a moment. Matthew smiles.)*

MATTHEW.   You know, I don't meet people. It's not that I don't get out — my wife and I do, we do get out — but I don't often, you know, as a general rule, just *meet people.*

CORY.   It's what I do for a living.

MATTHEW.   Really?

CORY.   Or, more specifically, *follow* people.

MATTHEW.   *(With a laugh.)* Follow them — why?

CORY.   It's my job. Deadbeat dads, cheating wives, runaway kids. I meet a lot of people — *(Extending her hand extended to him.)*

MATTHEW.   Matthew.

CORY.   *(Shaking his hand.)* An awful lot of people. And it's nice to meet *you.* How's the play going?

MATTHEW.   You're like a private investigator?

CORY.   I prefer "dick" — but its a phrase that's out of favor.

MATTHEW.   That's really wild. I've never — it must be — I don't know — I think I'd like to do something like that.

CORY.   You want to chase after misery day and night?

MATTHEW.   Well, it can't be all that bad — I mean you get to travel and —

CORY.   And I get to act, pretend to be things I'm not, just like

47

you —

MATTHEW. Well, yeah, right —

CORY. But the bullets are real and the deaths are final.

MATTHEW. Wait. You said you followed people, you didn't say anything about —

CORY. I follow them. And if I'm asked to do *more* than follow them ... I do what I'm asked.

MATTHEW. You carry a gun?

CORY. Don't you? *(She looks at Matthew gravely for a moment, then breaks into a large, warm smile.)* I like you, Matthew.

MATTHEW. *(Smiling with her.)* You know, you had me going there for a minute —

CORY. How is it, working with Adrian?

MATTHEW. It's — well, it's funny (not like laughing funny, more like maddening funny). We've been in rehearsal for a two weeks now. And nearly every day, just before lunch, he sends me out of the room. He closes the door. And he works on the scenes featuring my wife, Lisa.

CORY. Do you think they're going to run away together?

MATTHEW. *(With a laugh.)* Run away?

CORY. Yes.

MATTHEW. You mean like the Dish and the Spoon?

CORY. So, while they do that, you come here?

MATTHEW. Yes. But, usually there are waiters and food.

CORY. Why don't you stay and watch?

MATTHEW. He sends me away. He's the director and he can —

CORY. Why don't you stay and watch?

MATTHEW. You just said that.

CORY. Through a parted window blind. A door left ajar. Why don't you leave your coat behind with a tape recorder running? *(Pause.)* Don't you wonder what they're doing?

MATTHEW. They're rehearsing the play, I assume. I hope. What kind of question is —

CORY. Don't you wonder what they're doing? *(Matthew stares at her, then takes a very long swig of his wine.)*

It's odd. We think our lives will be changed in front of us — that we'll be present when it happens. But, we never are.

Our lives are changed in distant rooms. Without our knowledge or consent. Some word or glance, some quiet decision across town or across country is often the very thing which comes back and does us in.

Ignorance, Matthew, is not bliss.

It simply postpones the inevitable.

MATTHEW. You're gorgeous. *(A delicious pause between them.)* God, that felt good. Do you have more wine?

CORY. Sure. *(She hands him another small bottle of wine from her jacket.)*

MATTHEW. The thing about loving someone — this might turn into a speech, is that okay?

CORY. It's fine.

MATTHEW. — The thing about loving someone, over time, is that you start to feel the only way you can truly surprise them is to hurt them. That's terrible, I know, and avoidable, I suppose — but it hovers there, nevertheless. After some years together, you've spent all your compliments, dished out all your praise, used up a thousand "I love you's" and "I love you" variations, you've got a history of kind words and houseful of pet names — but you've lost the ability to *shock. (Leaning in to her.)* I don't know your name.

CORY. Cory.

MATTHEW. Cory ... you're gorgeous. (God, that rings when it's new.) But what could I say to Lisa, after all these years, that would carry the same weight?

I want out.

I'm leaving you.

I'm having an affair.

Surely there must be more options than that.

CORY. Are you having an affair?

MATTHEW. I don't know. Am I? *(He looks in her eyes. She stares at him. Then, she leans in very close to him ... reaches her hand toward his chest ... and removes a pen from his shirt pocket. She lifts a matchbox from the table and shakes it — it's empty.)*

CORY. They're even out of of matches. *(Using Matthew's pen, she writes something inside the box of matches.)* What's Lisa's last name, Matthew?

MATTHEW. Foster. Same as mine. *Why? (Cory closes the match-book. She slides it across the table to Matthew.)*

CORY. Now, you have my number. *(Stands, touching his cheek gently.)* As things develop, give a call. *(Suggested music: "Please Be Kind"* sung by Ella Fitzgerald. Cory puts on her sunglasses and leaves. Matthew watches her go, as lights shift to:*

ADRIAN'S HOTEL ROOM.

Adrian and Lisa are sitting on the bed, drinking red wine. Clothes loose, spirits high.)

LISA. I don't know. Am I?

ADRIAN. Not pissed, exactly. Not pissed, per sé. But, perhaps on the verge of pissed.

LISA. It's an awful word you people use — "pissed." I much prefer "drunk." It sounds more like what it feels like.

ADRIAN. American common sense strikes again.

LISA. I've no sense. *(She kisses him.)* No sense at all. *(She kisses him again.)* Did you see the paper this morning?

ADRIAN. No.

LISA. The hurricane is picking up speed.

ADRIAN. A new one, you mean?

LISA. Yes. It's headed straight for shore. Evacuations have been ordered.

ADRIAN. And what are they calling this one?

LISA. Adrian. *(Kiss.)* Adrian Ross. *(They hold each other. Music has faded out.)* Why did you divorce your wife? *(He stares at her, pulls away a bit.)* What? I'm sorry — is that a nerve? *(He continues to look away.)* Adrian, I —

ADRIAN. We divorced because I was a mediocre husband. And though my wife could tolerate that, I could not. I've been mediocre at many things in my life — my work as a director included — yes, you needn't say it, you needn't coddle me, I'm fully aware that I'm only half the director I wish to be. Thankfully it's a job in which one is encouraged to be an asshole, so I've done quite well for myself — but, in the case of my mar-

* See Special Note on Songs and Recordings on copyright page.

50

riage, I couldn't bear the weight of my own *common-ness*. The harder I looked at my life, the more I discovered how very *ordinary* I was. A tepid man, slogging through his days, hauling around the albatross of my own minutiae. *(Pause. Then, a laugh at his own expense.)* I'm sorry. I think it's the wine talking. Maybe we should —

LISA. Shut up and let the wine talk. *(She pours him some more wine.)* Where is she now? Your ex?

ADRIAN. I've no idea. She spent the greater part of our marriage trying to change into the woman she thought I wanted her to be. But, since I didn't know, really, who that woman *was* — she just ... kept on changing. So by the time I finally left her, I barely recognized her. *(Lisa looks at him. Then she removes her gold wedding ring from her finger.)* What are you doing?

LISA. We've only four weeks left. We must move with dispatch.

ADRIAN. And then? *(Lisa holds her ring up to the light, looking at it.)* When that time is over ... what then? *(She looks at him. Suggested music: "Am I Wrong?"* by Keb Mo — first verse, as lights shift quickly to:*

FRANK'S OFFICE.

Frank is making notes on the clipboard, as — Matthew enters, buoyantly, carrying a white paper sack from a deli. Music out.)

MATTHEW. Hello, Frank. Sorry I'm late.

FRANK. No problem. Were you out having a smoke?

MATTHEW. No, Frank. I've turned over a new leaf. *(Matthew removes two small salads in plastic containers from the sack. He hands one to Frank.)* Salad? I didn't know what kind of dressing you like, so I grabbed a bunch. *(Matthew drops a handful of packets of dressing into Frank's lap.)*

FRANK. Matthew, to what do we owe —

MATTHEW. I'm having an affair, Frank!

FRANK. Say again?

MATTHEW. An affair. A torrid affair. More about that later.

* See Special Note on Songs and Recordings on copyright page.

51

And you know what else: I got a tattoo. A huge RED HEART
— it covers my entire back. Hurt like hell. I'll show you in a
minute —

FRANK.   Matthew, what in the world —

MATTHEW.   And furthermore, Frank: Yesterday a guy cut me
off on the freeway. So I followed him. And I pulled him over.
And I *shot him to death.* He bled like a leaky garbage bag. You've
hardly touched your salad.

FRANK.   Matthew, I think we need to go back.

MATTHEW.   We went back.

FRANK.   *(Firm.)* No. Back to the beginning of this session. I
want you to stand up and get your thoughts in order and come
through that door again.

MATTHEW.   For you, Frank, anything. *(Matthew stands and
leaves. He immediately returns, saying —)* Hello, Frank.

FRANK.   Hello, Matthew. What's new?

MATTHEW.   *(Happily.)* I've been making things up! (But you
probably could tell — you're a professional, you've got plaques
on the wall.) I've been pretending to have an affair, get a tattoo, kill people who don't use their turn signal — things like
that. And, in doing so, Frank, I've had a breakthrough.

FRANK.   Of what sort?

MATTHEW.   I was walking to the deli just now and it hit me:
"Matthew, *maybe you're wrong.*" Amazing, isn't it? All these weeks
you've been asking me: "Are you *sure*, Matthew? Are you *certain*
that your wife is having an affair?" But, now I know that's not
my true fear, Frank.

FRANK.   It's not?

MATTHEW.   No, my true fear is this: that Lisa has stopped loving me. *(Pause, more quietly.) That* is my true fear —

FRANK.   *(Making a note.) Good*, Matthew —

MATTHEW.   And now, having named that, I see that all my
other fears are ILLUSIONS. *She is not sleeping with Adrian* — I
invented it!

FRANK.   Matthew —

MATTHEW.   I made it up!

FRANK.   Matthew, I applaud your realization, but that doesn't
mean your *suspicions* are necessarily *untrue* —

MATTHEW. ALL IN MY MIND, Frank. I've misconstrued EVERYTHING because I fear our love is gone. And, perhaps it is. And that will break my heart and I'll spend years with you in this stupid room. But, for now, this much I'm certain of: *there is no affair.*

FRANK. Matthew —

MATTHEW. *(Definitively.)* None at all. *(Frank stares at him, as lights shift quickly to:*

ADRIAN'S HOTEL ROOM.

A moonlit night. Adrian and Lisa are in bed, under the covers. Lisa's head rests on Adrian's bare chest. Her shoulders are bare and exposed. Suggested music: "Moon Love"* by Chet Baker, plays softly, under.)

LISA. Do you remember?

ADRIAN. Hmm?

LISA. When I met you — that first day — you passed me in the hallway. And you said hello. And then you said something else. Do you remember?

ADRIAN. Tell me.

LISA. You said: "Yes." And I looked at you — not knowing what you meant. And you said: "Yes is the answer." To what? I asked. "To whatever you'd like to do with me." *(A wry smile.)* You were such a prick.

ADRIAN. Yes. So you said. *(They kiss. They hold each other.)*

LISA. We've got to tell him, you know.

ADRIAN. How?

LISA. We'll sit him down. We'll look him in the eye. And we'll say — *(Adrian sits up in bed, saying —)*

ADRIAN. *That's* what I'm looking for.

THE REHEARSAL STUDIO.

(Bright lights once again. Music out, abruptly. Matthew sits at a distance, watching.)

* See Special Note on Songs and Recordings on copyright page.

53

ADRIAN.   Do you see now, Matthew? *That's* the quality the scene desperately needs. *(Adrian throws off the covers and gets out of bed. With the exception of his shirt, he is fully clothed. He pulls his shirt back on, as — Matthew glares at him. Lisa pulls her shirt or sweater back up over her shoulders.)* Try it yourself this time. And, please, keep in mind —

MATTHEW.   Adrian. May I ask you something?

ADRIAN.   Certainly.

MATTHEW.   Just how STUPID do you think I am? *(Quick beat.)* Let me rephrase that: Have you no SHAME? Do you think I'll just stand blindly to the side as you BED MY WIFE?!

LISA.   Maybe we should take ten —

ADRIAN.   Yes, let's do that — *(Calling to the Stage Crew.)* Let's strike the bed, please — *(The Crew strikes the bed during the following.)*

MATTHEW.   *Say it.* Both of you. Just *look me in the eye and SAY IT.*

LISA.   Matthew, what are you —

MATTHEW.   *(Sharp.)* You know perfectly well. *(Matthew quickly sets two chairs, side by side — identical to Act One.)* Let's do this. I'll go out and have a smoke. And when I return, you'll be sitting here, side by side. And you'll *tell me all of it.* Is that too much to ask?

LISA.	ADRIAN.
This is not the —	Matthew, listen —

MATTHEW.   Just SAY THE WORDS. *(They stare at him, saying nothing.)* Was it *good?* Is it *still* good? Will it be good *tonight?* Or maybe at *lunch* if you can give me the slip and steal an hour? Or *half an hour?* Or maybe just a *few minutes* — a few, protected moments alone to look in each other's eyes. To kiss. To bury your faces in each other's clothing. To put your tongues in each other's mouths. To *plot.* To whisper. *(Silence. Then, Lisa goes and sits in the chair, facing Matthew. Adrian does not move.)* Thank you, Lisa. Adrian?

ADRIAN.   *(A firm resolve.)* We are here to talk about the play. The play and nothing more. Do you understand?

LISA.   Adrian, please, there's no point in —

MATTHEW.   The *play?*

ADRIAN. Yes.

MATTHEW. And nothing more?

ADRIAN. Yes.

MATTHEW. You know, I *quite agree!* Let's work on the PLAY, shall we?!

LISA. Matthew —

MATTHEW. *(Taking her script from her.)* Could I look at your script, Lis? Thank you so much. I think I left mine at the office of my SHRINK during one of my INNUMERABLE SESSIONS to REHABILITATE my DISAPPEARING sense of SELF WORTH. *(Quickly, to Lisa, anticipating her question.)* Yes, I'm in therapy. Whoop-Dee-Doo. *(Opening the script.)* Now: Let's begin. Please, Mr. Director, advise us. Which scene shall we be undertaking today?

ADRIAN. The final scene.

MATTHEW. How fitting. C'mon, Lis. "This is how he works" — *you know that. (To Adrian, as he imitates Adrian's action of changing the angle of the chair ever-so-slightly.)* I'm, of course, happy to *use the chair* or *not.* Whatever you think.

ADRIAN. Now, as we've discussed, the affair between them is long over. The *entire thing* is in the past —

LISA. *Well* in the past —

ADRIAN. It's been *four years* —

MATTHEW. Yes. But, I wonder from, say, her HUSBAND'S point of view, if it really *is* over? Do the two of them really think he's been blind to EVERYTHING?

ADRIAN. I think they're operating under that premise, yes.

MATTHEW. *Interesting.*

LISA. *(Moving away.)* Shall we begin?

MATTHEW. One more thing: In the flashback scene — the one in which her husband first declares his love for her — Lisa's character says: "Be careful what you're getting into. I'm trouble." *(To Lisa.)* Do you know the scene I mean?

LISA. Yes, I do. He should have considered that before he married her. She gave him fair warning.

MATTHEW. But that's just the thing: When a man hears that a woman is "trouble" — he doesn't take it as a warning. He takes it as a *dare.*

LISA.   That's not her fault.

MATTHEW.   It seems *nothing is.*

LISA.   She was being truthful with him. Completely truthful. And she expected the same in return.

MATTHEW.   *(Laughs.) Complete truth?*

LISA.   Yes.

ADRIAN.   Matthew, I don't think Lisa is —

MATTHEW.   *(To Adrian.)* I'm sorry, but that would be brutal. *(To Lisa.)* You don't — your CHARACTER doesn't want that much truth. No one does. Truth as a RULE — yes. Truth MORE OFTEN THAN NOT — yes. But not ALL THE TIME. Any good mate knows the value of the *comforting little lie.*

LISA.   Such as?

MATTHEW.   Oh, in the case of her husband: What he really thinks of her FAMILY. Her FRIENDS.

LISA.   Hey, wait a minute, he LIKES her friends.

MATTHEW.   *(To Adrian.)* There's the BEAUTY OF LYING! She really believes it!

ADRIAN.   Let's get on with the scene, if we could —

LISA.   No, let's *address this.* MY character sees it differently.

MATTHEW.   *(Tossing the script at her feet.)* Do enlighten us.

LISA.   *(Not picking the script up.)* I think if you look carefully at the TEXT, you'll see that her husband lives in some kind of *dream world.* He can't stand the fact that his LIFE does not match his FANTASIES, his little THOUGHTS —

MATTHEW.   What are you —

LISA.   And not that she KNOWS his thoughts — not at all — how could she? — when *he won't let her in.* He wouldn't dare trust her with his thoughts — because that might SHOCK HER or SURPRISE HER —

ADRIAN.   Lisa, let's move on —

LISA.   He'd never PUT HIS HEART ON THE LINE FOR HER, because that requires *courage* — that requires —

ADRIAN.   Lisa, please, stop it —

LISA.   *(Turning to Adrian.)* And, then there's her lover. *(Pause.)* Or what *passes* for a lover in a *play like this.* His idea of courtship is to talk her ear off and then buy her a bathing suit the size of a *bookmark.*

ADRIAN. Lisa —

LISA. He thinks he can *chat* his way into her heart — but this man's got nothing to say. He's pure noise. This man is *noon at a clock shop!*

ADRIAN. That's QUITE ENOUGH —

LISA. Look at it, both of you: it's all a *dirty mess* and she's CAUGHT IN THE MIDDLE OF IT.

MATTHEW. *(Simply.)* That explains the showers. *(They both look at him.)* It seemed so *odd* to him that she began to take a shower every night before she climbed in bed with him. In all the years of their marriage, she'd never done that — until now. What did it *mean?* he wondered. Why this sudden need to be *clean? (Lisa stares at Matthew. Then, she picks up the script from the floor. Her voice softens, she moves closer to him — holding the script in front of them both.)*

LISA. If you do, though, look at the text … this is what you'll find: That when the affair is over and done with, four years later, *she returns to him. (From the script, softly.)* "So, it worked out?" he asks her.

MATTHEW. And she says —

LISA. "Yes."

MATTHEW. "Your marriage."

LISA. "Yes."

MATTHEW. "I'm glad for you. *(Pause, quietly.)* Really." *(He stares at Lisa. Then, he moves the chair out of the way, saying —)* You know, Adrian, I've always wished that — for the final scene of the play — the stage could be bare. *Completely bare.* Pared down to its essence. Leaving only the fundamental unit of human life: Two people. And time. *(He approaches Lisa.)* I've wished I could walk up very close to her.

And then — as the play ends — the two of us would attempt love's one true act of bravery:

To face each other.

To look into each other's eyes.

And to *not run. (He looks in her eyes. After a moment, Lisa looks away from Matthew, turns and leaves. Matthew watches her go. After she is gone, he turns to Adrian.)*

Have you had a nice month with my wife? *(Adrian is silent.)*

I don't blame you for loving her. She's a warm, smart, vibrant woman — and you know as well as I that without the likes of her, the known world is a parking lot.

I don't even care if you love her *better* than I do. That's for her to decide.

But never ... *ever* ... think you love her *more* than I. For that, my friend, will be your undoing. I promise you that. *(Matthew leaves. Pause. Then, Lisa steps back into the room, looks at Adrian.)*

LISA.   What did he say? Adrian?

ADRIAN.   It's so odd: I'm jealous of him. That he is your husband. That you go to his bed at night. Think of it — I'm jealous of a man whose wife is deceiving him, whose trusting heart is crumbling to ash. *(She stares at him.)* I'm still married, Lisa. I came to the States to hide, really. My wife had hired a private investigator to track my whereabouts in London. To gain proof of my indiscretions. *(Silence. Lisa speaks softly, reigning in her anger.)*

LISA.   Indiscretions. You mean, like, *lies? (Pause.)* Like telling me you're divorced? You mean, *little things like THAT?*

ADRIAN.   Lisa, listen to me —

LISA.   Well, you know something: you can add *us* to the list of things you're mediocre at.

ADRIAN.   I'm not alone in this, Lisa. You are —

LISA.   *Indiscretions.* Is that us? Is that who I am? Am I *this month's indiscretion?*

ADRIAN.   Lisa, please — *(Lights shift instantly to separate shafts of light on — Lisa and Frank. Frank holds the clipboard, pen poised.)*

LISA.   *(Urgently.)* I had a dream last night —

FRANK.   Tell me, Lisa.

LISA.   And in my dream I am washing dishes. I have taken off my wedding ring, as I always do. And I reach into the soapy water and pull out a little Tupperware container. And I remove the top. And there is a *heart* inside. A human heart, still beating. And in the dream I remember reading that a heart can live for about five hours outside the body before it dies —

FRANK.   Between four and six hours, actually, depending on age, condition —

LISA.   And I know that before it dies I have to find out who it belongs to — and return it to him. So, I seal it up in the Tupperware. And I get in my car. I go to Adrian's hotel room. I open the door. I reach inside his chest ... and his heart is there, pounding away. So, I drive home. And I look everywhere for Matthew. I drive to rehearsal. I check the restaurant, the book store, the deli. I can't find him anywhere. I go home and wait for him. I sit on the floor and stare at my watch ... holding the little container in my hands ... the heart beating ... the hours ticking away....

FRANK. And did Matthew ever arrive?

LISA. I woke up. *(Silence.)*

FRANK. The waiting is very telling. What are you waiting for, Lisa?

LISA. I'm waiting for —

FRANK. Yes?

LISA. I'm —

FRANK. Yes?

LISA. Let me *finish.*

FRANK. It's been more than a month —

LISA. I'm aware of that —

FRANK. Well?

LISA. I'm waiting for the right time.

FRANK. The right time to break it to him?

LISA. Yes. Is that so bad?

FRANK. Oh, I see. There is a *good day* to devastate someone?! Perhaps you'll wait till he wins the *lottery* and then tell him. Or wait till you're on your *deathbed* and then tell him.

LISA. You've made your point —

FRANK. Lisa: *the perfect time to hurt someone never comes. (Lights instantly restore to:*

THE REHEARSAL STUDIO.

Lisa and Adrian are exactly where we left them.)

ADRIAN. Lisa, please —

LISA. So I was, what, the person who looks after your feelings when you're on the road, away from home? I was, what, your *heart-sitter?*

ADRIAN.   I was going to tell you —

LISA.   When?

ADRIAN.   When the time was right. *(Silence.)*

LISA.   You should go.

ADRIAN.   Lis —

LISA.   Rehearsal is over. *(Adrian looks at her, then exits. Lisa sits on the ground in the center of the room. She closes her eyes, crying quietly, as, from behind her — Cory enters. Her hair is short and red, as before. She wears her leather jacket and sunglasses. She carries a leather shoulder bag.)*

CORY.   Pardon me. Sorry to disturb you, but — *(Lisa turns.)* I'm looking for a Lisa Foster.

LISA.   That's me.

CORY.   *(Removing her sunglasses.)* Really? *(Lisa nods.)* Lisa, I wondered if I could ask you a few questions.

LISA.   About...?

CORY.   It's a private matter. *(Cory produces an 8 × 10 photo of Adrian from her shoulder bag. She holds it out to Lisa.)* Do you know this man? His name is Derek. Derek Savage. He often directs under an alias: Adrian Poynter.

LISA.   I know who he is. *(Pause.)* His wife hired you, didn't she? To track him down.

CORY.   I'm not at liberty to say.

LISA.   Well you've found him.

CORY.   You're working with Adrian currently?

LISA.   Yes. I was his first choice. *(Pause.)* You can tell his wife it was me. Whatever information she needs, I can give it to you. *(Pause, stands.)* And ... stupid as it sounds, and inadequate as it is ... you can also tell her I'm sorry. I had no idea he was still married. Will you tell her that for me?

CORY.   I will. *(Cory is staring at Lisa.)*

LISA.   Is there anything else?

CORY.   I met your husband, Lisa. He seems very nice. *(Cory turns and goes. Lisa is alone for a moment. Then, Matthew enters. He walks directly up to Lisa and looks in her eyes.)*

MATTHEW.   *(Quietly.)* Lis. *(Pause.)* You can tell me the truth. *(Pause.)* It's all I ask. Just look in my eyes and answer me: Are you having an affair? *(A pause, then ...)*

LISA. *(Honestly, directly.)* Yes.

MATTHEW. *(Pause, quietly.)* Thank you.

LISA. With Adrian. But it's over now, Matthew. It's over and done. *(Pause, from her heart.)* I'm sorry. *(Frank appears in the room, holding Matthew's script — unopened.)*

FRANK. *Matthew?!* Is that really what she —

MATTHEW. Okay, NO, that's what I *wanted* her to say, and I know there's a DIFFERENCE — but right now I'm not —

FRANK. *(Firmly.)* Matthew — we've come this far together. Tell me what she *really* said.

MATTHEW. All right. *(Matthew pauses, turns back to Lisa — who has not moved.)* What she really said was:

LISA. *(Honestly, directly.)* No. Don't be silly, Matthew. I'd never do that.

FRANK. *Matthew?!*

MATTHEW. OKAY, SO I NEVER ASKED HER! *(Lisa exits.)*

FRANK. Why?

MATTHEW. Because it makes no difference what she says! I'm trapped by my own suspicions: If she says "Yes" — I'm proved right and DEVASTATED. If she says "No" — she's *lying* and I'm VINDICATED. I can't win, Frank!

FRANK. Matthew, for god's sake, stop *fooling yourself*. You've got to face facts, you've got to —

MATTHEW. HOW, Frank? In what way? What is it you want me to tell you?!

FRANK. *(Exasperated, turning away from him.)* People think there are things I want to hear. I don't know where they get that notion. I ask direct questions — and then watch glaciers form on the faces of — *(Matthew points to the script in Frank's hand.)*

MATTHEW. That's from the PLAY. Those are lines from MY SCRIPT. Why would you be saying —

FRANK. *(Opening the script.)* I've had some experience in the theatre *myself*, Matthew, and I think it may serve our purpose here —

MATTHEW. Well, then. You should come to rehearsal with me. I'm sure *Lisa would be thrilled to see you.* Are her SESSIONS with you going well?!

FRANK. Matthew, where did you get the idea that —

MATTHEW. I have a new friend, Frank. She's a dick. She follows people. She followed Lisa to your office.

FRANK. Matthew, the privacy of my clients is —

MATTHEW. Oh, right — that's *"confidential."* The words *"conflict of interest"* also sort of come to mind, don't they, Frank?!

ADRIAN'S VOICE. Okay. Great. Let's set up the RESTAURANT. *(Adrian approaches the stage from the audience. During the following, the Stage Crew enters and changes the stage into the Restaurant from Act One.)*

MATTHEW. We're not FINISHED HERE! *(Adrian ignores him, and goes about setting up the stage. Frank approaches Matthew.)*

FRANK. Do as he says, Matthew.

MATTHEW. Leave me ALONE, FRANK —

FRANK. Go *back to the restaurant.* Back to the *final day of rehearsal* — when it all unraveled.

MATTHEW. Enough, Frank — no more sessions —

FRANK. This is not a session, Matthew —

MATTHEW. *(To Adrian — who does not hear him.)* Can we take ten, please?!

FRANK. And it's not a rehearsal.

MATTHEW. But, Frank — *(Frank ushers Matthew away, saying —.)*

FRANK. This, Matthew, is *the thing itself. (Lights shift quickly to:*

THE RESTAURANT.

Lisa and Adrian standing together. The scene is identical to that in Act One — with one exception: no party hats.)

LISA. We have amnesia. We forget what we know. *(Adrian returns to the table and sits. Lisa stands, alone.) This* time, we think, unlike all the previous anguish and innuendo, *this time* the good-byes will have a grace to them. They don't.

They never will. *(Lights shift to another area of the restaurant:*

A WAIT STATION.

Again, identical to Act One. As Matthew arrives, Cory is removing her long black wig — revealing her short red hair underneath. During the

following, she takes off her waitress apron and puts on her leather jacket.)
MATTHEW. Cory?! What are you doing?
CORY. *(Tossing the wig to him.)* No more illusions, Matthew. No more playing games. Are they still at the table?
MATTHEW. Yes. And, the restaurant is empty again — just like the day I met you. How does that happen?!
CORY. I have an arrangement with the owner.
MATTHEW. You *what?!*
CORY. I like the adventure of revenge, don't you? The fever of it.
MATTHEW. Cory, what are you —
CORY. It's just as you said: the only way to truly surprise some-one is to hurt them. *(Matthew stares at her, baffled.)* Let's do it. *(Cory goes, and Matthew follows her, as lights quickly return to:*

THE RESTAURANT TABLE.

As Cory approaches, Lisa, not looking up, says —)
LISA. I think we need more wine.
CORY. Check the yellow pages under "Liquor." Hello, Mr. Poynter. *(Adrian looks up. He freezes. Cory sits in the chair between them, as she says —)* Mind if I join you? *(Cory looks up at Matthew, standing.)* Matthew? *(Matthew pauses, then brings a fourth chair to the table and sits.)*
MATTHEW. Yes. I think I'll use the chair. *(The four of them sit there, looking at each other. Cory smiles.)*
CORY. How nice to be together. You remember me, don't you, Lisa?
LISA. Umm —
CORY. There's no umm here. You told me about your affair with Adrian. *(Pause.)* I told you his real name was Derek. *(Pause.)* And you told me to tell his wife that you were sorry.
LISA. I am.
CORY. Well. I accept your apology. *(Lisa and Matthew stare at Cory.)*
MATTHEW. *(Softly.)* What?
ADRIAN. *(Simply.)* The hurricane has arrived. Lisa, this is

63

Cory. My wife.

CORY. *(Now: an impeccable British accent.)* Hello. *(Cory lifts a glass from the table and drinks.)* I think it's going very well. Don't you, Matthew?

ADRIAN. So, this is who you are now? *(Cory nods.)* I thought you'd hired a private eye.

CORY. Oh, love. Who could possibly track you down better than I? Lisa, dear, I have something of yours. *(Cory holds up Lisa's gold wedding ring. Lisa checks her ring finger, surprised that it's bare.)*

LISA. Where did you get — ?

CORY. I was going through my husband's hotel room. And there it was under the bed. *(Holding it up to the light.)* It's the simplest thing, you see. A *circle*. *(Giving the ring to Lisa as she looks at Adrian.)* Everything comes round. *(Cory pulls a gun from her leather jacket and points it at Adrian.)* Stand up. *(Matthew and Lisa stand and back away.)*

MATTHEW.	LISA.
Cory, what are you —	Oh, my god —

ADRIAN. Cory, PLEASE —

CORY. Quiet, love. You don't have lines in this scene. Move away from the table. *(Cory trains the gun on Adrian, who pleads with her.)*

ADRIAN. You mustn't do this, Cory —

CORY. Oh, *mustn't I?*

ADRIAN. Listen to me. It needn't be over between us —

CORY. Are you going to lie to me again?

ADRIAN. No, I'm not.

CORY. There! You lied again.

ADRIAN. Our lives could begin anew —

CORY. And again!

ADRIAN. I never intended to hurt you, Cory —

CORY. You *can't stop*, can you?! *(Matthew steps in, toward Cory.)*

MATTHEW. CORY, NO — this is not the way I remember it!

CORY. *(Turning to Matthew, with the gun.)* No, Matthew, this is the way it *happened*. *(Matthew backs away. Cory again returns the gun on Adrian.)*

64

ADRIAN. Cory — please — let me explain — *(Cory cocks the gun. Adrian kneels and grovels, quaking with fear.)*
CORY. *Just tell me when you can't take it, anymore.*
ADRIAN. I can't, Cory! I CAN'T TAKE IT ANYMORE! Please. Don't do this. I beg of you — *(Adrian has curled up into a ball on the floor, whimpering, terrified. Cory keeps the gun trained on him — shaking with rage — about to pull the trigger. Then ... exhausted ... Cory lowers the gun to her side, unable to shoot him. She sighs deeply, turns away from him.)*
CORY. *(Softly.)* Don't be silly, love. I could never hurt you. You know that. *(A long pause, as Adrian stands, takes a deep breath, collecting himself.)*
ADRIAN. Thank you. *(Cory quickly turns and fires, saying —)*
CORY. Good-bye. *(A loud gunshot which echoes for a long time through the room, as lights instantly isolate — Frank, addressing the audience. Frank holds the script — unopened — but does not refer to it. The sound of a distant siren.)*
FRANK. *Why?* — you may ask. I am asked that often. In this case, the common casualty was truth and the reason given was love. The bullet — like Cory herself — merely grazed Adrian's heart. No charges were filed. The wounds healed. And they returned, on separate flights, to London. *(The siren fades away.)* As for Matthew and Lisa: They stood side by side as the ambulance took Adrian away. Then they parted, saying nothing — and haven't seen each other in *years.* Passion and suspicion — they are twin fevers. Each blind us to this, the most obvious of facts: in time, everything gets known. *Everything.* And, in the end —
MATTHEW'S VOICE. Okay, great, thank you. *(Lights immediately expand to reveal:*

THE REHEARSAL STUDIO.

Identical to the beginning of the play. Matthew sits behind the table — wearing a change of clothes, to indicate passage of time. Frank opens up the script, pleading.)
FRANK. But, I'm not *finished* —
MATTHEW. I've seen all I need. Thanks for coming in —
FRANK. But, please, if you'd just let me —

MATTHEW. We'll call you when we know. Now, if you'd —
FRANK. *(Starting off, carrying the script.)* You didn't even give
me a *chance* —
MATTHEW. If you'd please leave the script behind, and —
FRANK. But, Matthew, I —
MATTHEW. *Drop it, Frank. (Frank stares at him, then drops the
script to the ground. Turns and leaves. Matthew enjoys throwing
Frank's resumé into the trash, then says —)* Next. *(Lisa enters. She,
too, is wearing a change of clothes. She stands in the room, as Matthew
makes a note in front of him — not looking up.)* Name? *(Lisa says
nothing. Matthew looks up, saying —)* I said — *(He sees her. Stops.
Speaks, quietly.)* Oh, my god. Lisa. It's been —
LISA. Years.
MATTHEW. Yes. *(Pause.)* Four years. And you're still —
LISA. Finishing your sentences. *(He smiles a bit. So does she. Si-
lence.)* So, it worked out? Going off on your own?
MATTHEW. Yes.
LISA. I'm glad for you. *(Pause.)* Really.
MATTHEW. And you?
LISA. Nothing to report.
MATTHEW. Four years? *(Lisa nods.)* And there's been no —
LISA. Only you. *(Silence. He stares at her.)* Something I've won-
dered. All that time with Adrian, you never — I kept waiting
for you to just *come out and ask me*, but you —
MATTHEW. No. Never. It's still your secret. *(Silence.)*
LISA. I'm here to audition.
MATTHEW. Lisa —
LISA. Just like old times. I'd like to do the final scene. I'd like
to have the ending you always wished for. *(Pause.)* The two of
us. And *nothing else. (Pause.)* Can we do that? *(Matthew takes a
long look at Lisa, then says, simply —)*
MATTHEW. Yes. *(Matthew snaps his fingers. As he does so — suggested music: "I Want You"* by Tom Waits. The Stage Crew enters and
removes everything from the stage. If possible, all other existing scenery
and masking — including the Rehearsal Studio itself is carried and/or*

* See Special Note on Songs and Recordings on copyright page.

flown away — leaving the stage [and theatre] as barren as possible. Matthew and Lisa watch, surprised, as the set disappears around them. Then, they turn to each other — the entire stage between them. Music continues under.)

LISA.   *(Quietly.)* What now?

MATTHEW.   I want to see your eyes. *(Lisa steps toward Matthew. He, too, steps forward — until they are facing each other at center stage. They look into each other's eyes.)* Do this.

LISA.   What?

MATTHEW.   Lie to everyone but me. *(Matthew and Lisa remain, face to face, looking into each other's eyes, as — The song concludes, and — The lights fade slowly to black.)*

END OF PLAY

AUTHOR'S NOTE

Private Eyes began as a lie.

Years ago I was sitting in a hotel room in Louisville, Kentucky, writing a scene in which two lovers fail to speak the truth. And, like a lie, the play grew. It began to go to greater and greater lengths to keep its own deceit afloat. It took my sense of structure for a ride and built a web of such complexity that clarity (aka "truth") was rendered virtually impossible. And even now, years later, sitting in a hotel room in Tucson, I think back to that first scene and say to myself: it started so simply. Doesn't it always.

I have a friend who assures me that he is incapable of jealousy. He has convinced his wife of this fact. I admire him for this. I envy him this. And I don't — in my heart's heart — believe him for a minute. Jealousy is part of love's arsenal, with suspicion as its fuse. And though I agree with Camus' adage that "no man has ever dared describe himself as he is" — I have tried to write about my own fascination with the high-wire act known as "an affair": the insidious power of suspicion, the delicious fever of deception ... and the accompanying sobriety of truth. For beneath the headlines of our heartache lies something quieter, simpler: the fear of loss. The failure of love to answer its own promise. The low-level panic of two people, alone, looking in each other's eyes, with nowhere to run. Nothing between them but distance. Nothing awaiting them but time.

A play about lies must be a comedy, because only laughter can make us recognize truths we're not fond of. Only laughter is generous enough to hear us out, to listen to our foibles and our familiar debacles ... and let us think that next time, *next time*, it will be different.

Thanks for taking the ride.

— Steven Dietz
5 April 1996
Tucson

PROPERTY LIST

Actors' resumés (MATTHEW)
Shoulder bag with thermos of tea (LISA)
Resumé (LISA)
Scripts (LISA, MATTHEW, ADRIAN, FRANK)
Pad of paper (MATTHEW)
Pen or pencil (MATTHEW, ADRIAN, FRANK)
Sunglasses (MATTHEW, CORY)
Papers (MATTHEW)
Menu (MATTHEW)
Wristwatch (MATTHEW)
Pen (LISA)
Glass of red wine (LISA)
Matchbox with 1 match (MATTHEW)
Knife (MATTHEW)
Covered plate with full box of matches (LISA)
Bills (money) (MATTHEW)
Folded script pages (MATTHEW)
3 glasses of red wine (MATTHEW, LISA, ADRIAN)
Plastic noisemakers (CORY)
Paper party hats (CORY, PHOTOGRAPHERS)
Cameras (PHOTOGRAPHERS)
Tray of salads with dressings on the side (CORY)
Glass of water (CORY)
Small, glass vial with yellow powder (MATTHEW)
Fork (CORY)
Pepper (CORY)
Severed end of a pay phone (CORY)
Long red rose (CORY)
Clipboard (FRANK)
Freshly sharpened pencils
Coffee mug (ADRIAN)
Newspaper (LISA)
Small, airplane-size bottles of red wine (CORY)
Empty matchbox (CORY)
Wine bottle (LISA, ADRIAN)
Wine glasses (LISA, ADRIAN)

White paper deli sack with 2 small salads and packets
        of dressings (MATTHEW)
Leather shoulder bag with 8 × 10 photo (CORY)
Wig (CORY)
Gold wedding ring (LISA, CORY)
Gun (CORY)

SOUND EFFECTS

Distant, eerie music
Manic laughter, amplified
Gunshot
Siren (distance and fading)

NEW PLAYS

- **SMASH by Jeffrey Hatcher.** Based on the novel, AN UNSOCIAL SOCIALIST by George Bernard Shaw, the story centers on a millionaire Socialist who leaves his bride on their wedding day because he fears his passion for her will get in the way of his plans to overthrow the British government. *"SMASH is witty, cunning, intelligent, and skillful."* –Seattle Weekly. *"SMASH is a wonderfully high-style British comedy of manners that evokes the world of Shaw's high-minded heroes and heroines, but shaped by a post modern sensibility."* –Seattle Herald. [5M, 5W] ISBN: 0-8222-1553-5

- **PRIVATE EYES by Steven Dietz.** A comedy of suspicion in which nothing is ever quite what it seems. *"Steven Dietz's ... Pirandellian smooch to the mercurial nature of theatrical illusion and romantic truth, Dietz's spiraling structure and breathless pacing provide enough of an oxygen rush to revive any moribund audience member ... Dietz's mastery of playmaking ... is cause for kudos."* –The Village Voice. *"The cleverest and most artful piece presented at the 21st annual [Humana] festival was PRIVATE EYES by writer-director Steven Dietz."* –The Chicago Tribune. [3M, 2W] ISBN: 0-8222-1619-1

- **DIMLY PERCEIVED THREATS TO THE SYSTEM by Jon Klein.** Reality and fantasy overlap with hilarious results as this unforgettable family attempts to survive the nineties. *"Here's a play whose point about fractured families goes to the heart, mind -- and ears."* –The Washington Post. *" ... an end-of-the millennium comedy about a family on the verge of a nervous breakdown ... Trenchant and hilarious ... "* –The Baltimore Sun. [2M, 4W] ISBN: 0-8222-1677-9

- **HONOUR by Joanna Murray-Smith.** In a series of intense confrontations, a wife, husband, lover and daughter negotiate the forces of passion, lust, history, responsibility and honour. *"Tight, crackling dialogue (usually played out in punchy verbal duels) captures characters unable to deal with emotions ... Murray-Smith effectively places her characters in situations that strip away pretense."* –Variety. *"HONOUR might just capture a few honors of its own."* –Time Out Magazine. [1M, 3W] ISBN: 0-8222-1683-3

- **NINE ARMENIANS by Leslie Ayvazian.** A revealing portrait of three generations of an Armenian-American family. *" ... Ayvazian's obvious personal exploration ... is evocative, and her picture of an American Life colored nostalgically by an increasingly alien ethnic tradition, is persuasively embedded into a script of a certain supple grace ... "* –The NY Post. *"... NINE ARMENIANS is a warm, likable work that benefits from ... Ayvazian's clear-headed insight into the dynamics of a close-knit family ... "* –Variety. [5M, 5W] ISBN: 0-8222-1602-7

- **PSYCHOPATHIA SEXUALIS by John Patrick Shanley.** Fetishes and psychiatry abound in this scathing comedy about a man and his father's argyle socks. *"John Patrick Shanley's new play, PSYCHOPATHIA SEXUALIS is ... perfectly poised between daffy comedy and believable human neurosis which Shanley combines so well ... "* –The LA Times. *"John Patrick Shanley's PSYCHOPATHIA SEXUALIS is a salty boulevard comedy with a bittersweet theme ... "* –New York Magazine. *"A tour de force of witty, barbed dialogue."* –Variety. [3M, 2W] ISBN: 0-8222-1615-9

DRAMATISTS PLAY SERVICE, INC.
440 Park Avenue South, New York, NY 10016 212-683-8960 Fax 212-213-1539
postmaster@dramatists.com www.dramatists.com

NEW PLAYS

• **A QUESTION OF MERCY by David Rabe.** The Obie Award-winning playwright probes the sensitive and controversial issue of doctor-assisted suicide in the age of AIDS in this poignant drama. *"There are many devastating ironies in Mr. Rabe's beautifully considered, piercingly clear-eyed work ... " –The NY Times. "With unsettling candor and disturbing insight, the play arouses pity and understanding of a troubling subject ... Rabe's provocative tale is an affirmation of dignity that rings clear and true." –Variety.* [6M, 1W] ISBN: 0-8222-1643-4

• **A DOLL'S HOUSE by Henrik Ibsen, adapted by Frank McGuinness. Winner of the 1997 Tony Award for best revival.** *"New, raw, gut-twisting and gripping. Easily the hottest drama this season." –USA Today. "Bold, brilliant and alive." –The Wall Street Journal. "A thunderclap of an evening that takes your breath away." –Time. "The stuff of Broadway legend." –Associated Press.* [4M, 4W, 2 boys] ISBN: 0-8222-1636-1

• **THE WAITING ROOM by Lisa Loomer.** Three women from different centuries meet in a doctor's waiting room in this dark comedy about the timeless quest for beauty -- and its cost. *" ... THE WAITING ROOM ... is a bold, risky melange of conflicting elements that is ... terrifically moving ... There's no resisting the fierce emotional pull of the play." – The NY Times. " ... one of the high points of this year's Off-Broadway season ... THE WAITING ROOM is well worth a visit." –Back Stage.* [7M, 4W, flexible casting] ISBN: 0-8222-1594-2

• **MR. PETERS' CONNECTIONS by Arthur Miller.** Mr. Miller describes the protagonist as existing in a dream-like state when the mind is "freed to roam from real memories to conjectures, from trivialities to tragic insights, from terror of death to glorying in one's being alive." With this memory play, the Tony Award and Pulitzer Prize-winner reaffirms his stature as the world's foremost dramatist. *" ... a cross between Joycean stream-of-consciousness and Strindberg's dream plays, sweetened with a dose of William Saroyan's philosophical whimsy ... CONNECTIONS is most intriguing ... Miller scholars will surely find many connections of their own to make between this work and the author's earlier plays." –The NY Times.* [5M, 3W] ISBN: 0-8222-1687-6

• **THE STEWARD OF CHRISTENDOM by Sebastian Barry.** A freely imagined portrait of the author's great-grandfather, the last Chief Superintendent of the Dublin Metropolitan Police. *"MAGNIFICENT ... the cool, elegiac eye of James Joyce's THE DEAD; the bleak absurdity of Samuel Beckett's lost, primal characters; the cosmic anger of KING LEAR ..." –The NY Times. "Sebastian Barry's compassionate imaging of an ancestor he never knew is among the most poignant onstage displays of humanity in recent memory." –Variety.* [5M, 4W] ISBN: 0-8222-1609-4

• **SYMPATHETIC MAGIC by Lanford Wilson. Winner of the 1997 Obie for best play.** The mysteries of the universe, and of human and artistic creation, are explored in this award-winning play. *"Lanford Wilson's idiosyncratic SYMPATHETIC MAGIC is his BEST PLAY YET ... the rare play you WANT ... chock-full of ideas, incidents, witty or poetic lines, scientific and philosophical argument ... you'll find your intellectual faculties racing." – New York Magazine. "The script is like a fully notated score, next to which most new plays are cursory lead sheets." –The Village Voice.* [5M, 3W] ISBN: 0-8222-1630-2

DRAMATISTS PLAY SERVICE, INC.
440 Park Avenue South, New York, NY 10016 212-683-8960 Fax 212-213-1539
postmaster@dramatists.com www.dramatists.com